MIND SHIFTS IN HEALTHCARE

Proven Employer Strategies to Bend the Cost Curve and
Improve Employee Health, Well-being and Engagement

Dr. Wade Larson

Mind Shifts in Healthcare: Proven Employer Strategies to Bend the Cost Curve and Improve Employee Health, Well-being and Engagement

ISBN: 9781074216191

Independently Published – KDP Publishing

This book is dedicated to the HR and business leaders trying to find ways to help employees afford quality healthcare to improve quality of life.

Strategies to Bend the Cost Curve

Contents

BENDING THE CURVE.. 1

Bending the Healthcare Curve.. 3

The Moral of the Story 10

The Unsustainable Curve of Healthcare 13

When Does Healthcare Becomes Helpful?.. 15

But…We're Not in The Business of Healthcare............................. 16

Healthcare Reform is Local: Stop Waiting.................................... 17

Why Accountable Care Organizations Don't Work 18

Why Accountable Care Organizations Might Work........................ 20

Understanding Costs: Primary Drivers 21

Claims 21

Stop Loss.. 22

Pharmaceuticals.. 23

Medical Inflation 23

Regulation 24

Litigation... 24

Employer Reactions to the Curve: Mitigation 26

Creating a New Mindset... 28

FOUNDATIONS OF STRATEGY 31

Foundations of Strategy... 33

What Do You Want? 33

Why Do You Want It?.. 35

How Do You Get It? 36

Your Strategy is for YOU.. 37

Your Goal…Putting Health in Employees' Hands 39

Change Management... 40

Step 1: Create a Sense of Urgency...................................... 40

Step 2: Build A Guiding Coalition 41

Step 3: Form A Strategic Vision and Initiatives 41

Step 4: Enlist A Volunteer Army 42

Step 5: Enable Action by Removing Barriers 42

Step 6: Generate Short-Term Wins 43

Step 7: Sustain Acceleration 43

Step 8: Institute Change 44

A Multi-Year Approach 45

Example: Integrated Wellness Program 46

A Multi-Constituent Approach 56

Care 56

Adopters 57

Incentives 58

PARTNERSHIPS 61

You Cannot Do This Alone 63

Internal Partnerships 64

Guiding Coalition 64

Executive Team 64

Selling Wellness 65

Wellness Committee 67

Employees 68

Spouses and Dependents 69

External Partnerships 72

Brokers 72

Carriers 73

Vendors 73

Providers 76

STRATEGIES TO CONTROL THE CURVE 81

Take Control – How Employers Can Do Something 83

Continuous Improvement 85

Continuous Improvement as the Tool 85

Step 1: Identify Where You Are 87

Step 2: Evaluate Against Your Vision 90

Step 3: Plan 92

Step 4: Execute 93

Your Vision & Strategy 95

Initial Assessment: Starting Point 95

Budget 98

Structure & Plan Designs 101

Self-Funded vs. Fully Funded 101

High Deductible Plans 102

Funding Mechanisms – HSAs 104

Your Education Strategy 108

Wellness: Selling the Benefits 113

Financial Managers: Challenges to See the ROI 114

Employees: Challenges to See the Results 115

Meaningful Rewards Based Program 117

Wellness Committee 121

Outcomes Based 122

Activities 124

Promoting "Wellness Your Way" 124

Creating Options 124

One Example: Integrated Wellness at Wagstaff, Inc. 128

YEAR 1: WELLNESS ROLL-OUT 129

YEAR 2: SELF-FUNDING/WELLNESS INTEGRATION 129

STEP 1: TOBACCO 129

STEP 2: WELLNESS (PPO) 130

STEP 3: WELLNESS (HIGH DEDUCTIBLE) 130

STEP 4: INCENTIVES 131

SUMMARY 132

NEW MINDSETS 133

Doing Things Differently 135

Welcome to the Game 136

A New Mindset 136

Pharmacy Carve-Out 137

Medical Tourism 139

Direct Billing Relationships 143

Pharmacy Tourism 144

Stop Loss Captives 147

Chronic Disease / Targeted Condition Programs 149

Diabetes Management Program 149

International Mail Order Scripts 150

Direct Primary Care / Onsite or Near-Site Clinics 151

Addressing Chronic Conditions 151

Onsite Clinics 152

Near-Site Clinics 153

Third-Party Providers 154

Telemedicine and Telehealth 155

Value to an Employer 155

Value to an Employee 156

Virtual Behavioral Health 159

Telephonic Health and Lifestyle Coaching 159

Coupons 160

SUPPORT STRATEGIES 163

Support Strategies 165

Personalized Experiences 166

Data Analytics 168

The Problem with Data 168

Your Source of Data 168

Nutritional Counseling 171

    Ideas for Including Nutritional Counseling 172

Lunch and Learns 175

Weight Management Programs 177

    Why the Employer Influences the Most 178

    Goals of Your Weight Management Program 179

    Ideas to Start the Conversation and Engage 180

    Wade's Journey 184

On-Site Gym 188

On-Site Trainer and Participatory Classes 189

Integrated Wellness 190

Other Ideas 191

Introduction

Healthcare is the #2 expenditure on your books – second only to payroll. Do you treat it as overhead or an investment? If it's an investment, what is your ROI and how do you measure it?

I have pondered just how to start this book to capture your attention and make you catch my energy, attitude and approach to sharing my perspectives.

The traditional start to the story of "healthcare is a challenge" just sounded boring and is an understatement that makes me laughable as an author.

Yet when I tell the truth – "managing healthcare sucks!" – it may come across as being unprofessional. However, it seems to just cut to the chase and summarize what we're all feeling, doesn't it?

Let's go with that.

No matter what we do, there seems to be no end to frustration. We try to manage costs, but the costs keep going up. Our best efforts to promote healthy living only result in seeing the belly lines grow around the office. Claims grow, behavior worsens, and we wait for the next legislative move to put an undue burden on us as an employer to offer just "one more thing" to put us in the poor house. It's downright infuriating some days.

Those of us who have been around the past few decades have seen the debacle of "healthcare reform" that only results in the insurance companies making more money. In what other business do you see the prices rise so quickly, the quality decrease, availability shrink, costs of services continue to increase, and have so many variations to price?

The truth is that employers are looking for solutions. You are looking for options of ways to make healthcare work that is affordable and effective.

Why Write the Book?
I am in the current round of matching the right people with the right strategy with the right resources and the right momentum – again.

The result? We're saving a lot of money – millions a year. This allows us to cut costs for employees while improving access to affordable healthcare. Is it perfect? Not yet, but it frees up financial resources to help us address many of the solutions plaguing employees, their health and barriers to longevity.

I cannot take all the credit. The credit goes to exceptional leadership who recognized that there was a problem and didn't need to know how to solve the problem. They only needed to recognize there was a problem and loosen up the resources to find the solution. When these powers align, people get excited to become part of the solution.

We have a lot of "someone oughta's" in this world…the ones who sit around saying "someone oughta do something to fix that." The same goes with healthcare. Someone "oughta" fix it. We rely on government and society to do something. How's that working for us?

We need to move from "someone oughta" to "I'm gonna". When that happens, we can move into the world of GSD – Get Stuff Done. We can clarify the necessary steps to make things work, who to utilize, and continuously improve processes. As we do, we streamline procedures that get in the way and simply sit down with the employee walk through the process.

That said, I'm writing this book to share what I know with you. It's not laid out perfectly and I am guaranteed to leave something out. However, it is meant to be a guide of "best practices" and "lessons learned" that have worked for me multiple times. The lessons and topics are worth millions if implemented. They're worth nothing if left alone. Your choice.

My Goal
My goal each time I use the model is simple:

BEND THE COST CURVE OF HEALTHCARE!

I'm not so naïve as to think I can reverse the curve. However, in my most recent experience, there was enough of a spread with a negative trend lasting for several years in a row that I am almost a believer that it may be possible to reverse it. I won't get ahead of myself.

First thing's first. I want to help you understand what it takes to reform healthcare for your organization and provide options to reduce costs for your employees. You may have heard some of these ideas in the past – but are you doing them? All of them? It's going to take a lot of work, but it does not take a huge team. My team has always been small and busy with so much more. Healthcare has never been my full-time job. It has, however, always been a key consideration and one of my largest "wins" because of the impact it can have to your bottom line.

Caveats

While I alluded to it in the introduction and I continue to do so throughout the text, let's clarify that the statements in this book are all mine. The comments, discussions, recommendations and conversations all originate from me. *Nothing in this book is intended to nor should it be construed to reflect the opinions, policies or directions of any company for whom I work, have worked or have ever performed work.* The opinions and perspectives are my own.

Let's also clarify a few things as you prepare for your journey of reading the materials:

- I tend to be less formal as I discuss these points. Yes, I have the credentials and could have written with more formality, but this book is meant to be one professional sharing what has worked for me through the years. If I wanted to write a formal textbook I would have done so. I am instead writing a book wherein I share best practices of what has worked for me through the years.

- This book is written directly – from me to you. I have few (if any) references and citations to external sources. This is "Dr. Wade's Recipe" to saving millions on healthcare. If you want a long list of resources and references, there are many books on the market with those resources. Unfortunately, they are written by people who did some research, slapped some facts together and are telling *other people's* stories. I'm telling you what works from decades of making it work first-hand.

- These solutions may not work for you. They may seem too crazy or they may seem like they are not enough. That's up to you to decide for yourself. I make no promises and no guarantees as a matter of practice in this book. The ideas presented are just that – ideas. They do not hold magical properties that, when applied, will automatically result in anything.

- Nothing that I suggest in this book can work by itself. Each idea presented must be used in tandem with the other core functions and activities that are central to the program. No single activity presented within this book will in and of itself be your saving grace.

- Everything I present here is part of a multi-faceted, multi-year process. There are no quick fixes that will save you immediately. If you just opened your renewals and you're looking for a way to get out of trouble, this book will not give you many ideas for mitigation. However, it will give you several ideas on what to start working on for next year.

- Lastly, if you don't try these ideas, and it doesn't work, you have no room to complain. I hear comments about my program that run the gamut from several folks that these ideas are "too edgy," "too simplistic," "old school," and that they'll "never work." What I know is that if you try nothing, you'll get nothing. What I also know is that I've done this more than once and each time I have had a demonstrable ROI within the first year worth a million dollars and worth several more times that within the first few years. The principles work.

With the caveats in place, let's get started with our journey.

BENDING THE CURVE

Bending the Healthcare Curve

INTRODUCTION

If you keep doing what you've been doing...

Employer-sponsored health insurance covers about half of all insured Americans. Understanding that many Americans pay for insurance out of pocket and the government covers the cost for Medicare, Medicaid, Tricare, state programs, and other forms of insurance to cover the other half. This makes the American employer the single largest payer into the costs of medical premiums into the system.

Unfortunately, most employers treat health insurance as a cost to be managed and mitigated...something that will "happen" to them. Most employers are reactionary when it comes to healthcare, waiting for the renewals each year and praying that the claims and medical trends will "not be that bad".

As a critical stakeholder in the "healthcare ecosystem," we as employers are essential to putting together plans, programs, and covering costs. Yet we have limited our influence, pressure, and voice when it comes to wellness, disease management, claims, and contract negotiations with insurance companies. As employers, we have far more influence than we know.

That said, we've been talking about "healthcare reform" and other strategies to address the incredible costs of healthcare for decades now. But what has changed? If you're like most employers, you do the same thing...receive the dreaded envelope at renewal time from the broker and roll the dice hoping for the best.

While you may rely on this strategy as your first approach to controlling costs, remember...

HOPE IS NOT A STRATEGY.

(Well, it's not a good one anyway.)

3

Strategies to Bend the Cost Curve

Once you receive your annual renewals, there is nothing you can do about it other than mitigation. You can attempt to negotiate the rates down, but other than that it's an effort to (a) pay for the increase, (b) share the cost with employees, or (c) cut your benefits further so you can afford health insurance just one more year.

How many years can you continue to do this before your health insurance is no longer a benefit? Their premiums go up, deductibles go up, out-of-pocket goes up, co-pays go up, coverage goes down, and even with insurance they can no longer go to the doctor when they are sick. As a result, your employees come to work ill and get others sick at work. They miss work, impact productivity, become injured more, take longer to heal (thereby impact absenteeism and productivity even further), and result in more worker compensation claims. When the patient does finally go to the doctor, he/she waited longer than they should have to go, so the claims are much larger than they would have been if they had gone sooner (as much as 10x or more. Think I'm kidding? Try treatment for influenza vs. hospitalization for pneumonia.)

Suddenly, your "cost savings" don't make as much sense as they did when you were trying to fit it into that renewal budget.

There MUST be a Better Way

You would think by now that someone has come up with a better way to do this…that someone would have figured out a way to make this work. Do you want to know the dirty little secret? Many have…and they have been telling us for years how to make this work. Unfortunately, we have been dismissing these ideas for the past two decades. Why?

- **They're too simple**. Some of these strategies are so simple, many dismiss them, thinking "that can't be the answer" when in fact, they are.

- **They sound too crazy**. I have many conversations with people who tell me that some of these ideas are just crazy. I admit…they may be…but my employees love them. And then I show them my reserve account — the conversation about "crazy" ends.

4

- **They require some work**. Yes, they do, but remember…we're managing the SECOND LARGEST EXPENDITURE on the balance sheet for most companies. Yes, it deserves some time.

- **They require buy-in**. This effort cannot be a one-person project that is mandated. Systems that work will require buy-in from the top and the front line (your employees).

- **They require outside-of-the-box thinking**. You hate that cliché, I know, but it does require something that is outside of the norm because what we've been doing isn't working. Period.

- **They require a bit of initial discomfort**. Here's the secret. Nobody likes to BE changed, but nobody minds changing IF they think it's THEIR idea…so the secret is to provide the incentives, motivation and inspiration to make the change their concept. Then reward the heck out of them for making the changes that benefit the plan.

- **They require leadership**. Someone needs to raise the banner, wave it, and drive the change. It won't happen on its own. The brokers won't bring this to you. Your carriers won't bring this to you. The healthcare providers are not going to be the change agents. And the government will NOT be the agents of change. Look…HEALTHCARE REFORM COMES FROM WITHIN. You need to be the one that drives it…someone does…and that takes leadership, pure and simple.

- **They require a bit of "guts"**. OK, a lot of guts. It's going to feel lonely at first because you'll be messing with perhaps the most sacred benefit that you offer. Nothing is more personal than health insurance because you affect people's lives with this, sometimes even more than changes to salary. This gets personal, so it's going to take some guts to make changes…but you can make life a lot better, a whole lot faster with their help.

Every time I share what I am going to share in this book, I hear the list of excuses as to why it won't work. When the HR manager brings the CFO to the table and I explain the system, the most common response is, "I just can't make the numbers work."

Well I have…more than once. It's not that hard, just a lot of work. It's like any other predictive indicator. You reap what you sow – you cannot harvest first and then promise to plant. Nothing works that way. The CFO of all people must know that it is impossible to obtain returns on investment if there is no investment. Still, because the methods I discuss are somewhat less-than-linear or the approach is subjective, there is a sense of doubt that creeps in and casts doubt on the whole thing.

Just like any new game that you have learned to play, you must trust that the better you understand how to play the game – the better you know the rules, the strategies, and the resources – the better the outcomes. Managing healthcare is no different.

Welcome to the Game

When I talk to people about healthcare, I often refer to it as a "game". Due to the cost and impact associated with this so-called game, many colleagues take offense to my reference as a find it to be somewhat unprofessional. If that's the case, so be it. The reason I referred to it as a game is because just like any other game, if you know how to play the game – the rules, strategies, and how to make the most of your players – you have a better chance of winning. If you don't know the rules, you don't use strategies, and don't care about the players, you will lose… EVERY TIME.

Sure, even if you know all the rules, strategies and players, there are times when you have bad years. Someone will be diagnosed with cancer, someone will have a major traffic accident, a trend of illnesses will hit that will increase your claims, or something else may happen that will drive your costs up that are out of your control. That might happen. At the same time, if you don't know the rules, play the game effectively, and utilize the best strategies, you will have a lousy year EVERY year and continuously fight to survive for your very existence.

While that occasional bad year sneaks up now and then, trends demonstrate that if you do the right things and manage your plan well, those happen on a rare occasion. If the program works well, you can absorb those years when they do come up. Trends and research also show that if you fail to manage your plan effectively, it will manage you – and when the bad years hit, they will be catastrophic.

The people who learn and play the game the best are the ones who win. The employers who understand the game and educate their employees so they become full partners are those that have the greatest success. Just like any sports team, when the team owners, coach and players are all on the same page, communicate openly, understand how the plays work in the team strategy, there is a higher chance for team success. The same thing goes for this game we call healthcare. As we bring everybody on board – educate them, explain things to them, and bring them on as *real* partners - they can then work with us to achieve better outcomes.

A Choice to Play the Game

We have a choice and we don't have a choice. Let's start with the choice that we don't have - to offer healthcare. If you are an employer with more than 50 employees, you are required by law to provide affordable healthcare. While the laws change periodically, this rule is not going to go away anytime soon for two reasons. First, offering healthcare to your employees is a good idea. When people do not have healthcare, bad things happen and society pays for it anyway. It's a burden on families, it's a burden on society, and it has catastrophic impacts on the people who can afford it the least. (I won't touch the social ramifications of not having health insurance for the general public – and don't worry, this is coming from a conservative perspective.)

The second reason is that it will continue to be required by law. This rule started with the Affordable Care Act (Obamacare). Even after the Obama administration, with some of the changes that continue to take place, the mandate to carry health insurance by an employer remained. It is something that is desired by employees and many employers, and it probably will not go away at all under any administration.

Outside of the social and legal reasons for offering healthcare is the choice to provide it …primarily for competitive purposes. This may affect those of you who have fewer than 50 employees as well. Even though you may not be required to offer it, you may give it some thought to either provide it directly or to subsidize their premiums out in the marketplace. The competition for talent (labor, employees, etc.) is fierce. There are too many jobs for the number of people available. This trend will continue for many years into the future. Offering benefits – especially healthcare benefits – becomes a competitive advantage. For

7

professional positions, it is a standard. For hourly jobs, it becomes a competitive advantage that may serve you well.

While healthcare is expensive, it is something that we as employers must take into consideration as something good for business. Keep this in mind: healthy employees are happy employees, happy employees are productive employees, and productive employees are effective employees who get the job done. If you want an effective company – that meets expectations, achieves goals, and is profitable – that requires employees who do the same. That doesn't happen with people who are overworked, underpaid and are generally unhealthy. Offering a health plan that incorporates workplace wellness can help to support a vibrant and high-performance workforce that can help you achieve your company goals far more effectively than trying to save a few bucks by going cheap on health insurance.

Why I Know This Works

To get to the point, I have worked with the companies who implement these practices and bend the healthcare cost curve. Each time, it has saved the organization millions in claims that lowered and the premiums that they didn't have to pay year after year. I'll share more examples as we go through the book, but the principles are the same and they are sound.

The first time was in a comfortable situation – public sector, a fully-funded PPO plan that they had little reason to do it. We shifted over to a wellness-based program using a health reimbursement plan (HRA) as the funding mechanism for incentives since we couldn't use an HSA in a PPO program. While we had only experienced an average of 6% rate increases, that adds up over time. Within a year, that rate dropped and we experienced three years of 0%, 0% and 1% rate increases before I left. Compared to a consistent annual increase of 6% or higher, you can do the math on what that saved over time (don't forget to apply the cumulative effect of those cost savings over time!!!). These results happened without carving out **any** benefits and rewarding employees up to $2000 each for wellness incentives.

Another round is going on right now. Facing double-digit increases year after year, the company nearly doubled its healthcare spend in only four renewals. Applying several of the strategies that discussed in this book, we've had 4 years of negative trend, shifted to a self-funded model, have a cash reserve with millions, **increased** coverage for employees, and we decreased the rates for the third year in a row for our employees (costs are almost half of what they used to be for employees at all price ranges). In fact, with the HSA plan, employees and their spouses can earn their entire deductible back through wellness incentives. We're now even offering nearly free premiums to employees, so when combined with their ability to earn the entire deductible back through wellness incentives into their HSA accounts, the answer is YES...you can make this work.

The Moral of the Story

The principles of effective healthcare management and wellness are not rocket science. They are fundamental principles that work. As you read this book, you will come across some concepts that you will think are basic, rudimentary and simple. There are other things that you will consider to be silly or even dysfunctional. There may be some things that are unique, interesting or amazing to you. However, everything included in this book has been tried and tested in a real company setting. These are examples of programs that have been implemented and have worked in a practical setting. When many of these programs and concepts combine, they can work synergistically – where they work better together than the total of their outcomes.

The point is this. I do not expect anyone to read this book and implement everything. This book is a compendium of different ideas from different sources and approaches that I have used. Most of the processes outlined in the book come from my personal experience and application. They have been tried and tested successfully in my workplaces over the past 25 years. I share what it takes to succeed and pitfalls to be aware of that may cause failure. There may be some programs when in combination will not work together. I tried to point those out as well.

I hope you can identify a few concepts that you may be able to implement in your workplace. Even if you think of one good idea that could help to make a difference in someone's life, this will be worthwhile. The hope is to allow you the opportunity to brainstorm, collect new ideas, and figure out ways to adapt those ideas to your current setting. As you do, I am confident that you will be able to find the solutions you're looking for and then share them with others.

Here's to your success…

Mind Shifts in Healthcare

Strategies to Bend the Cost Curve

The Unsustainable Curve of Healthcare

When Does Healthcare Becomes Helpful?

It's unclear whether there were actually "The Good 'ol Days" when it comes to healthcare in America. Many of us remember back to times of low or no copays, deductibles, or coinsurance. Many can remember back to days of $0 cost sharing on premiums – insurance was "free." For many working professionals, healthcare was just something we got as a part of the employment contract. If we got sick, we went to the doctor and it might have cost a few bucks for a copay and a couple of dollars for the medicine.

Nowadays, it feels like we must take out a bank loan just to go to the doctor. As employees, it can easily cost $500-1,000 or more each month for the employee's portion of the insurance premiums (after the employer pays another $1,800 for us on a family plan). We end up with $1,500 - $4,000 or higher deductibles with $50 copays or 20% coinsurance. When we go to the doctor the first time during the new plan year, we cough up $250 for the office visit (until the deductible is met), another $150 for labs (until deductible is met), and then get a prescription that can cost us $60 with a copay. Maybe we're the only ones asking this question, but...

WHEN DOES OUR INSURANCE BECOME A BENEFIT?

It seems challenging, and when we look at history it's apparent that we can't continue to do what we've always done. I recall a series of double-digit increases back in the 90s, thinking, "this surely cannot continue – it's unsustainable!" Here we are several years later still saying the same thing. Consider what has happened over the past 60 years as demonstrated through a display of our national health expenditures per capita over the past several decades:

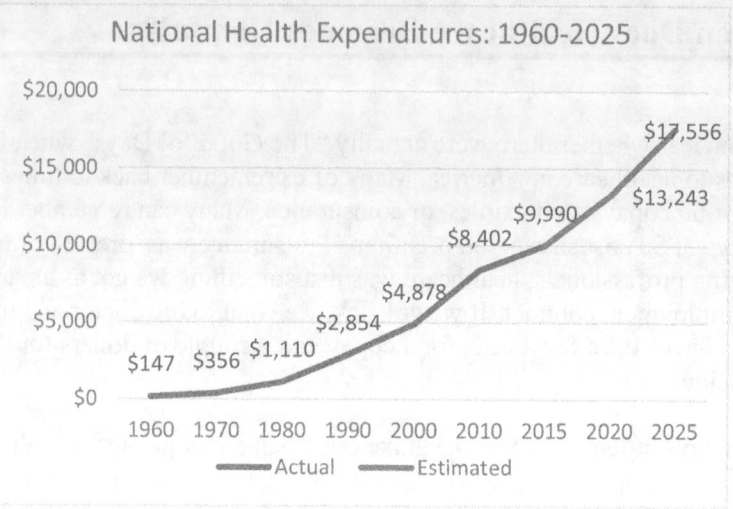

Sources: Centers for Medicare & Medicaid Services

But...We're Not in The Business of Healthcare

Yes, You Are...

Health insurance is typically the second largest line item expense for any company, regardless of whether the company is manufacturing or service based. This expense costs millions a year, and we should manage like it is. You have essential positions that oversee operations that are worth far less than the total value of your health insurance cost, watching over revenues and expenses, ensuring efficiency and effectiveness to provide cost savings or controls. Without the same level of care and concern for benefits, you'll never be able to bring this under control.

The good news is that employer-sponsored health plans are positioned in a way to grant you flexibility. You can usually adjust and pivot in your plan design, investments and approaches that allow you to make necessary adjustments as you go to balance cost and value. In the case of self-funded plans, you have even greater flexibility to make the changes needed to align the needs of the business with the program. This flexibility is unavailable in most other investments and cost centers you own as a business.

Healthcare Reform is Local: Stop Waiting

This entire book can be about nothing more than healthcare reform and why it doesn't work. The bottom line is this...the topic is one that will continue to be battled out in the media and politics. And the result? The same as it has been for the past three decades. Nothing.

It's a sexy topic in the sense that everyone wants to fix it. It's not very sexy in that no one has a solution that will work for everyone. You have people in Congress that have no idea what they are doing, without any experience in managing insurance, influenced by lobbyists working for special interests, making decisions to appease those with the loudest voices. Unfortunately, employers have NOT been among those with the loudest voices - the ones paying the most significant part of the health insurance bill are the furthest away from any solutions surrounding healthcare reform.

I'm not dismissing the efforts of some employers and individual groups who have tried. However, businesses each have their own agendas and their own ways to address their individual needs. There is no way to bring us all on the same page when it comes to reforming and controlling healthcare.

There have been legislative "solutions" to try to control costs, such as the Affordable Care Act which has done nothing to control healthcare costs nor has it made healthcare more affordable. Mandates to cover everyone to create larger risk pools have increased costs for the healthy and reduced accountability to the unhealthy in many cases. Sure, it has expanded coverage in many areas that have been beneficial to many (e.g., removing pre-existing conditions, eliminating lifetime maximums, expanding dependent coverage to age 26). Little has been shown to demonstrate the reformative impact of the efforts.

One solution that came from the ACA was to create Accountable Care Organizations (ACOs). The intent was to provide incentives and funding to streamline the cost of care and improve the quality of the delivery of care. Unfortunately, it was not clear how to do that. It was left to thousands of providers trying thousands of ways to chase a thousand approaches to make it happen without clear guidance on outcomes.

Why Accountable Care Organizations Don't Work

Healthcare organizations may demonstrate their efforts over the past several years to create ACOs. According to the ever-so-expanding networks of mergers and acquisitions that absorb the hospitals and private practices, ACOs are a solution to increase quality and reduce costs through better performance metrics.

From the business side of that statement, I am waiting to see the *actual* performance and outcomes because the ACO model has yet to show anything but ongoing cost increases and decreased service availability. Under the mantra of moving to an ACO model, networks have used vast cash reserves to absorb hospitals and private practices as fast as they can.

This caveat (or criticism) may sound cynical, but it comes from experience. As I sat on the board of a local health network a few years ago just as a representative of the business community, the CEO of the local hospital actively campaigned for the steps the hospital was taking to become an ACO. Each meeting moved forward with electronic medical record (EMR) projects and the costs associated with it, followed by complaints about the challenges he faced because the other providers in the area were either not moving to EMR or were using a different software platform. Soon, the conversation started to move towards new practices that would become part of the hospital's "network". After a bit, talks began to emerge about sister hospitals creating a "network".

At that time, I leaned over to the President of the health network and asked him if he saw what the hospital CEO was doing. He said "no", but probably did so as a courtesy. I told him, "I've got 5-bucks that says you're out of a job in 2-years because the hospital is creating their own network. I have another 5-bucks that says that in 10 years from now, nearly every private practice is taken over by these guys." Of course, he told me "no way" because that could never happen to this network that had been around for nearly 20 years to help control the costs of healthcare in the area and had done a great job thus far under his leadership.

He was out of a job in a year and a half. The existing network dissolved.

18

And 10-years later? It may be more than 90% of the private practices that are owned by the hospital group. In fact, because of the financial structuring and lucrative nature of healthcare (yes, I skipped the term "profitability" for a non-profit venture), they were able to take over several hospitals and private practices in the neighboring region over the 10-year period.

Did this help with cost containment? Not that I can see…the medical trend is still on the rise. Quality is the same. Access is still a challenge as it becomes harder to get an appointment, especially with a specialist.

For the ACO, the argument for them is often streamlined administration and lower overhead. To the end user – my employees and their families – it is typically fewer available appointments available to see a provider, less time with the actual doctor (and more time with a nurse practitioner or physician's assistant), and far less personalized service than before. While the Gen Z group may appreciate the automated kiosk to check them in at the doctor, my 60-year-old employee is lost when facing a machine and no one to assist them as they attempted to check in for their pathology appointment.

Does this mean that everything about the ACO push is terrible? No. The move to EMRs was inevitable. Healthcare could not continue to work in a paper world. ACOs may have been a catalyst in some cases to generate momentum towards digitizing records. However, like everything else in business, we may have been able to arrive faster and cheaper without the regulation and overhead involved with another layer of compliance involved with the Affordable Care Act.

With all the talk of streamlined costs and greater efficiencies, I have yet to see any proof that the ACO model has done anything that wouldn't have otherwise emerged. There may be an ACO out there that works and if so, great. I'm not here to argue that it's all bad…ACOs look great on paper. This perspective is one person's opinion that – at the end of the day, in BUSINESS-EZE terms – the ACO model in general HAS NOT DELIVERED on its promises. It has only driven up costs as it continues to spend money, take over smaller practices and conglomerate services, and reduce available access to necessary services for employees and their dependents.

Why Accountable Care Organizations Might Work

After all that, I see why some employers are considering and building direct contracting services and creating quasi-ACOs through transparent billing arrangements. That is part of the promise of the ACO model (a small piece of it). However, specific employers such as the City and County of San Francisco as well as the California Public Employee's Retirement System say they are creating a direct ACO contract for state employees. Given the level of bureaucracy built into those systems, I'm not hopeful that they will emerge as having streamlined anything.

Other larger employers are looking to create their own ACOs, however. The idea is sound with mega employers building their own ACO to organize, deliver and manage healthcare to their own employees and their dependents. To be honest – IT MAKES A LOT OF SENSE. We probably should have put business (the #1 payer of healthcare costs) in charge in the first place to find a more streamlined solution to make this work more efficiently instead of having government drive it through regulation. Unfortunately, we in business are so busy competing with one another that we cannot take a few moments to work together to come up with a common solution that will benefit all of us in the end.

When you think about it, a business venture where businesses partner with healthcare to streamline administration, modernize delivery, use data and analytics to ensure the best care and control costs, align strategies with performance, create pay and incentive structures for providers that align with outcomes, and all the other "promises" of ACO, it aligns with business. I'm eager to see if the business ACOs can make it work. Left alone, government entities are not the right ones to regulate ACOs into existence.

The hospitals have a lot of know-how on how to deliver good care. Businesses have a lot of know-how on how to streamline business and overhead for service delivery. The right care, the right service, at the right cost? Hmm…it might work.

Just one person's boots-on-the-ground perspective of the ACO debacle.

Understanding Costs: Primary Drivers

Before we can understand how to "bend" the healthcare cost curve as an employer, it is essential that we know what goes into those costs. It is not a magical number that some broker pulls out of a magic bag or that your insurance company provides. It is a projection of the anticipated cost of care and related expenditures throughout the year. Some direct considerations and expenses affect the cost of healthcare. There are also contributors – things that impact the costs. If we can understand where these costs come from, we can better understand how we can have an impact on those costs through our efforts.

Let's consider the primary drivers of healthcare costs for an employer relative to the health insurance program. If you're fully insured, you will typically pay a single check to the health insurance company each month based on a per employee / per month (PEPM) fee to cover all the costs, so everything is well hidden. If you are self-funded (and we're grouping partially and fully self-funded into this category), you typically have three or four bills you pay.

In both cases, you pay for the same things. They are just structured differently. Let's dig in just a little bit.

Claims

As my broker likes to tell me, "the claims are the claims." These attribute to the primary cost of health insurance for a company. Even in the marketplace, the aggregate claims of everyone covered on the plan are a primary consideration when determining the rates. The claims are the direct costs attributed to the goods and services (including pharmaceuticals, which we'll talk about separately) associated with employees getting care.

Why is this important to understand? Because insurance is insurance – the more you use, the more it costs. Let's take car insurance for example. We do our best to avoid accidents because if we crash, our rates go up. We also try to avoid speeding tickets and fines for the same reason.

21

While they are not accidents themselves, they are indicators of higher risk, and the insurance rates reflect the higher risk.

In the case of health insurance, when we wreck our bodies (like wrecking our car with car insurance), we use more services – which in turn increase our rates. Additionally, when an insurance company considers the group they are covering, they take the overall health and wellbeing of that group into consideration. Even if the group does not have a history of higher costs, if the group members demonstrate risky behaviors, it affects the price.

So, the bottom line is simple. Like anything else –

- The fewer goods and services you use, the less you pay.
- The less frequently you hit insurance with claims, the lower the cost.

If we really want to start getting control of healthcare costs, we need to get a hold of claims by (a) reducing the reason for having claims (e.g., getting people healthier) and (b) finding ways to make the claims less expensive (e.g., finding less costly ways to treat the claims with high quality care).

Stop Loss

Almost all groups have a stop loss insurance as part of their premium to help cover high claims (completely self-insured plans may set aside funding for this purpose even if a "premium" is not identified). It serves as secondary insurance that covers the costs of a situation that exceeds the point of the stop loss coverage. This level is typically between $75,000 - $150,000 but may be higher or lower. The lower the point, the more expensive the stop-loss insurance because it has a higher probability of being met.

Like claims, the more high-cost claims that hit the stop-loss insurance, the more it will cost you to maintain that coverage. It is a good thing to have this insurance – it's essential. There are some things (heaven forbid) that you cannot control, such as genetic conditions, car accidents, cancers, and other life-threatening conditions. The key is to prevent what you can and to mitigate what you can't.

Costs associated with stop loss depend on the group experience and varies, but it is *not* inexpensive. That said, whether stop-loss coverage is a primary driver depends mainly on your experience. If you have had good experience in the past, stop loss may account for about 10% of your overall costs on average for the year. If your experience is "less than optimal", trying to find stop-loss insurance at all may be a struggle, and if you do, the cost may be significant depending on past claims.

When considering the role that wellness plays – keeping your healthy people healthy (top priority) and helping your marginally healthy become healthy (second priority, but lowest hanging fruit in terms of improvement) – you see the impact it can directly play on costs. The fewer the claims that hit your claims, the lower the impact on the long-term costs on immediate claims projections as well as stop-loss calculations.

Pharmaceuticals

I talk about prescription drugs separately because of the size of their impact. Prescription drug funding is by far the fastest growing expense on your medical bottom line. With each new prescription drug that arrives on the market, many new patients will flock to it for aid. If it is a specialty drug, those prescriptions can cost $5,000, $10,000 and even more per month. The company that develops the medication tries to recoup the costs as soon as possible and maximize the profits while it still has the proprietary protection for the first 20 years before generics arrive. These costs are especially impactful on the U.S. market.

The costs of pharmaceuticals will continue to skyrocket in the years to come and it appears that there is nothing we can do about it. There are strategies that we'll talk about later in the book to control costs related to prescription drugs, but we as individuals and employers do not appear to have any control over what companies charge for these drugs.

Medical Inflation

Each year your health insurance accounts for inflation that takes place in the marketplace. The cost of medical equipment goes up, health care providers receive raises, and their business insurance costs increase each year. In addition to all the other expenses involved with providing healthcare, an annual "Medical Trend Rate" is calculated by various consultants, brokers and market watchdogs to estimate anticipated costs.

Trend is the trend. What it means for your group is separate. Your carrier and all parties with their fingers in your pocket will determine what it means to you and your bottom line. The less attractive your plan looks based on YOUR trends, YOUR utilization, YOUR population, and YOUR efforts, the more you will pay. Medical inflation is an indicator from the marketplace of what to expect and carriers will use it to justify additional inflation to your bottom-line costs. In the end, however, the real impact of medical inflation as a primary driver of your specific costs is nominal. It's used as more of a gauge to measure your performance against the "norm" and they will take your overall performance indicators into account when they evaluate.

Regulation
Many regulations govern health insurance. Each state will also vary regarding the rules that must be followed by health insurance companies and employers who sponsor health insurance plans for their employees. Regulations may include state taxes, federal taxes, and other fees. Additionally, employer plans must also pay PCORI fees (Patient-Centered Outcomes Research Initiative) under the Affordable Care Act. Several states require taxes, fees and other costs that become built into the base costs that may be non-negotiable. Some may apply to fully funded plans where additional charges may apply to all programs. Be sure to check with your broker about specific taxes and fees that apply to your plan.

Litigation
While built into the medical trends, we should note that there is no shortage of litigation from medical malpractice lawsuits, suits against pharmaceutical companies, etc. Any evening of television will have several advertisements asking to call if you have taken a medication and had poor outcomes. Someone must pay these costs, and that someone is each consumer of health insurance.

Also, keep in mind that your price includes these costs. At the point of service – the doctor's office, the checkout at Walgreen's – those prices have built in a margin to cover insurance specifically for litigation and costs associated for legal action. You're paying for it many times through the process.

Summary

In summary, the preceding was a VERY simplified conversation about some of the critical drivers of your claims. It is not meant to provide detail…that can fill a textbook. I am trying to make a point…not trying to derail us from the critical conversation of the book.

If we were to summarize the critical points of this section about costs, they would be this:

- There are costs you can control and costs you can't control.

- Of the costs you can control, claims are (a) the costliest and (b) the most controllable through prevention.

- The employer who is most familiar with what is driving their specific costs the most has the best chance of controlling the costs.

Find the opportunity to dig into your costs and claims. Run the analysis on your cost breakdown. When you evaluate claims, find out _exactly_ how much they cost and the trends behind them. Remember:

You can't fix what you don't know.

Without a good understanding of what is driving your cost, how will you know what programs and strategies to put into place to manage your costs and provide solutions?

Employer Reactions to the Curve: Mitigation

As the scriptural passage reads...

"If ye are prepared, ye shall not fear."

The employers who understand their cost structure and are actively managing it can plan and proactively put programs in place to address conditions and situations contributing to these costs.

Everyone else facing renewals typically braces for the impact of high costs. Year after year the business budgets for increases. However, it can only afford so much and when revenue does not increase at the same rate as health insurance, it has a choice – accept a reduction in profitability because it will now cost more to employ the same number of people or do something to mitigate the costs to the point that it fits within the budget.

In those cases where companies are merely responding to costs – waiting for the renewal envelope and then trying to figure out what to do to fit the renewal into the allotted budget – the *most common* mitigation strategies come down to three options:

1. **Cut Services**
    Each plan is different. The more things a plan covers, the higher the risk of use of those services and thus the higher the cost. In cases where an employer is looking to cut costs, they may look at what is covered and make cuts. For example, rather than 48 therapeutic treatments a plan may reduce options to 12 treatments. Rather than covering advanced treatment such as bariatrics, the employer may eliminate those services, and employees are left to themselves to pay for those services out of pocket.

2. **Cut Financial Coverage**
    While related to cutting services, cutting the level of coverage is another popular method to reduce costs. For example, rather than a $20 copay an employee may be charged $30. Instead of a $500 deductible, it may rise to $1,500. Costs of prescription drugs

may go from $10 generics to $20. Rather than paying only an office co-pay for advanced imaging (e.g., an MRI) a plan may change to a 20% copay structure.

3. **Share the Cost**
   Instead of or in addition to carving out benefits and coverage, an employer may also choose to pass along some or all the increase to employees to pay.

Employers are finding that because these have been the only solutions used for the past several years, these may be reaching their limits on availability and practicality. There is only so far they can go before the cost sharing becomes more than unreasonable.

No matter the option an employer chooses, the first reaction to health care cost increases is mitigation – to manage the costs to the point that the plan and its cost "fit" within the allowable parameters. It is a reactionary option as it becomes a "wait and see" approach to healthcare – waiting to see what the next renewal looks like and making crucial business decisions around that objective. This approach is simply a reactive approach to surviving the healthcare crisis. *Survival is not a healthy strategy.*

Employer Reaction to Crisis: Live with Disaster?
The healthcare crisis in the United States is without a doubt a disaster. The ongoing increases in cost are unsustainable. Currently health insurance represents the second largest single cost for most employers (surpassed only by payroll). As insurance costs rise faster than revenue, each employer must decide what long-term strategy will work for them. Continuing to use a mitigation-based approach to manage healthcare is an option – but *it's not the best case* in any scenario. Instead, employers can consider other options that can help them control the costs and bend the curve of this healthcare crisis.

Creating a New Mindset
At this point we probably haven't shared anything you don't know – but what have you tried to solve it? If you are still using the same strategies that you've always tried, you'll continue to get the same results.

It's time to try something new. This will take a new mindset to make this work.

Creating a New Mindset

I refer to the definition of insanity: doing the same thing and expecting different results. We can laugh all we want but think about your approach to managing healthcare. How different is it really? What are you doing differently today from what you were doing 5 years ago? What about 10 years ago?

Costs continue to rise despite our mitigation efforts.

Employees cannot take on any more cost sharing. You cannot go to the CFO or Executive Team and ask for another 14% to cover next year's increase. You wonder what next year's state and federal legislature will add to the new taxes and fees while the brokers, TPA, and other vendors increase their fees by a "nominal" 3% each year. Whether we suffer from accumulated "cost creep" or demonstrable years of bad claims, the insanity has led us to *a point of crisis*.

It's time to set aside subtlety.

If you want massive change, *you must take massive action*.

I recognize the balance – you cannot implement disruptive change too quickly or it will face resistance and rejection by the ones who need to adopt it the most. However, worrying about how to earn 100% adoption to make everyone happy will get you nowhere. At some point you will be asking questions about your ability to continue to offer benefits. In fact, you may be asking questions about the ability to keep your business running due to overhead costs.

By now you should be asking key questions. The natural question is IF it is possible to cut costs and find solutions that can deliver quality care, save everyone money, and be successful. That, unfortunately, is the WRONG QUESTION. We must adopt a different mindset because IF is NEVER THE QUESTION.

A new mindset calls for us to shift over into the world of "HOW". This presumes that the IF is a given. It's never *if*, but rather *how* you can achieve your goal. I am confident that you can and that is why we're here – to show you the "how's", but it will take a new approach. Let's start.

Strategies to Bend the Cost Curve

FOUNDATIONS OF STRATEGY

Foundations of Strategy

The start of every great outcome is a good strategy. That doesn't mean that you need a perfect plan...just a functional one that works for you. Every organization is different, and each group has its unique challenges when it comes to healthcare. While most would agree that the cost of healthcare is challenging, the "why" of those costs differ. For some it is access to healthcare while others are facing an increase in claims due to poor health.

If you are like most companies, your strategy may come a few weeks before the renewals arrive. Perhaps you give it some thoughts before that...about budget time, when you try to pull out the crystal ball and look ahead to do your best to guess how much your increase will be for the coming year. Whether it be at budget time or renewal time, it then becomes a tug-of-war between HR and the CFO to decide how much the company can afford, how much will be passed along to employees, and how many benefits will be cut to fit it into the budget.

Unfortunately, this is not a strategy. As a result of this so-called strategy, costs are high, benefits are barely beneficial, and plans cover less and less each year, leaving employees frustrated, companies broke and conditions untreated. Employers buckle in for double-digit rate increases, employees pay hundreds of dollars each paycheck for premiums (and thousands in deductibles and copays per year), and doctors make it challenging to schedule an appointment for anything less than 3-4 weeks out. Is there any question that the system does not work?

No matter where you are starting, there are some key questions that you must begin with to set the tone for your plan. Let's consider the building blocks to your program.

What Do You Want?
Let's start your strategy with an essential question:

WHAT DO YOU WANT?

This question becomes your driving purpose as you build and design your healthcare strategy. Most will ask me "What do I need to **DO** to

33

achieve success?" If I gave you a list of things to do, you'd have a nice list of "stuff" that may or may not work, but without a context to work within, that list is just a list and will not get you where you want to be.

Starting with, "What do you want?", create your list of what you want as a result of your healthcare strategy and program.

Most employers are going to put "money". Look…if money is your primary driver, your strategy will never work. If employees figure out that the only reason you want to run your program is to save the company money, that really won't excite them to make the changes necessary to make a difference.

Saving money is good. We all want to do it…but what will you do with it and how do you transport you there? Those are questions that will follow.

That's not to say that saving money shouldn't be one of the wants. It's a good want…it's a great desire. You may also want to consider…

- **Employee Health and Wellbeing**: Healthy employees are happy employees, and happy employees are productive employees. What's more, when employees are well and productive, they miss less work, are injured less, and stay with your company longer. Those are facts.

- **Spouse and Dependent Health**: Dependent claims generally run about half and often more of your total claims. Healthy families affect your bottom-line. When families are well, employees miss less work to take care of them and are less distracted when they are at work.

- **Employee Savings**: A commitment to saving employees money is a commitment to helping employees achieve a better lifestyle. Money and cost become personal. As they help you save money, a true partnership requires you to help them save money…at least those who help you achieve your goals.

- **Reward Contributions**: It is not uncommon to create a risk/reward situation where you reward those individuals who disproportionately support your efforts. Those employees who participate in your programs such as wellness, HSA plans, biometrics, etc. can earn substantial incentives, significant premium discounts, and other rewards that amount to thousands a year over those who do nothing to help your goals.

Why Do You Want It?
The next question to consider is your "WHY?" The "why" establishes your purpose and lays the foundation for your entire plan. Without a solid "why" and purpose for your plan and structure, you are still only chasing the next dollar and that can only last so long. With the right purposes in place, you can establish a plan that can create the structure for future growth while maintaining the flexibility required to grow and adjust as your plan matures and evolves.

Consider the following:

- **Employee Health and Wellbeing**: If your "why" is primarily focused on employee health and wellbeing, you create a proactive approach to health. You first and foremost take care of your employees…and when they know that you legitimately care about them, they will care about you. Sure, in the end they will be healthy, and that will help them to be a more productive employee, as well as reduce future claims. However, it is the right thing to do to help employees live a better life.

- **Family Health and Wellbeing**: Similarly, when we take care of the family, that is one less thing for which an employee will have to have to worry. It builds commitment and loyalty for an employee and they are appreciative to you the employer for what you provide to them and their family. Similarly, it will save money in the short-term and long-term, but more importantly, we take care of our employees and what is important to them.

- **Save Employees Money**: I suggest promoting the opportunity to put money in employees' pockets. If you can improve their health, reduce utilization by helping them to make smarter decisions (e.g., Telemedicine over the Emergency Room for a fever at 2 a.m.), and manage costs better, it's going to start to have a positive impact. At that point, you need to share the

35

"love" with them, so they feel the impact of their decisions through premium savings, reductions in deductibles, minimizing copays, and other measures to put more money in their pockets.

- **Save the Company Money**: Here's something to know. Why you want to do the program and what you communicate to others as to why you want to do the program may not be the same thing. If you want to save money for the company so you can hit quarterly earnings, great…this can help over time to mitigate costs. Employees won't care. If you want to save money so you can increase the employee bonus pool, you have their attention and commitment. Get it?

How Do You Get It?

The final foundational strategy element is "HOW". This step is where you fill in the blanks with what you and your company plan to do to fulfill your strategy for the year. That said, you can build the strategy, but if you do not pull it out to review it, use it, and have it guide your actions throughout the year, nothing will happen.

The rest of the book will give with specific ideas and concepts, but there are three primary considerations that you must consider as you develop your core strategy.

- **Internal Partnerships**: Internal coalitions will be essential to make this work. You cannot do it alone. If you want this to work, there are vital partnerships that you must develop, nurture and grow.

- **External Partnerships**: Your ability to take on something as sophisticated as healthcare requires a partnership among the players in healthcare including carriers, providers, brokers, vendors and others. Not only do they need to work for you, but they need to work together. We'll share more!

- **Education**: A key strategy to make this work is to make your employees effective consumers of healthcare. As they become more educated in healthcare, how it works, and how to find the best prices and deals, they'll begin to work FOR you in saving the company and plan money.

- **Wellness**: We share this over and over…the number one driver of cost in healthcare is claims. Healthy employees don't become sick, so to lower claims, let's focus on improving and maintaining the health and wellbeing of our employees and their families.

- **Best Practices**: Many employers have figured out many solutions. As an employer, you don't have to reinvent the wheel. Often, it's about finding the right strategy that works for you. Not every plan will work for every organization. At the same time, I can't cover everything in this book. Some of you may read this book and say, "Why didn't you include the XYZ Strategy?" Well, I didn't. I included a lot…but maybe I'll add it in the next book… There are so many opinions. Some will work. Some won't. Some are just crazy…and some are logical. I'll share several of them.

- **New Mind-Sets**: If the Best Practices section isn't enough, we'll venture into the new ideas that employers are trying out to combat the costs of healthcare. Some of these ideas are new. Some have been around for a while but are still "new" to people. Some are just crazy, I admit! But they are working for employers and this is the opportunity for you to ask the question, "What if???"

Your Strategy is for YOU

Remember…I'm not saying that you must do anything other than to do what works for you. Your strategy is yours. However, as you can imagine…

If you keep doing what you've always been doing, you'll keep getting what you've always been getting…

The same applies to healthcare. You can think about it, analyze it, debate it, or set the book aside. You'll keep receiving the same results as you always have. OR…you can take an idea or two and see if it will work.

However, the more you do, the more you receive. The more significant the investment, the bigger the rewards potential. Something is better than nothing, but more is better than less when it comes to the ROI of wellness.

Your Goal...Putting Health in Employees' Hands

Looking ahead 20 years from now, where do you want to be?

Here are trends to work towards as you build your program to make it useful. Knowing that change must happen at the claims level...the individual level, the local level...individuals must OWN their healthcare. They must be empowered, enabled, motivated and accountable to do what it takes to make the right choices, change their behavior and contribute to the overall success of the program. Here are some characteristics of the new program design that will make your program the most effective.

- Self-Service

- Choice Friendly...Health and Wellness *Their* Way

- Value-Based Program Design According to Individual Needs

- Multi-Channel Delivery of Services

- Rewarding to Those Who Help (Consumer Friendly, Incentives)

- Costlier to Those Who Don't Help

- Educational

- Accessible

- User-Friendly

- Value-Focused – Cost, Quality, Outcomes

- Automated

- Data-Driven

- Cool

Change Management

"Change happens when the pain of staying the same is greater than the pain of change..."

Tony Robbins

Understand that a new mindset will require change – and effective change requires change management. There's no better change management model than that provided by John Kotter. I have effectively used his change model when implementing this transformation and it has worked. I may not follow every step in the right order, and I may not follow every element to the degree in which the change management model requires, but let's consider our fundamental transformation applied to the Kotter model.

Step 1: Create a Sense of Urgency
Without a shared sense of urgency, the change will not happen. As the leader of this transformation, it is essential that you come up with a shared sense of purpose behind the change to create the momentum. Saving money for the company is never enough. Sure, it's a good starting point of the conversation but it is never enough to start the ball rolling and maintain the momentum for the type of change that you will need. It takes more than that.

"If the rate of change on the outside exceeds the rate of change on the inside, the end is near."

-Jack Welch

When I walked into my latest situation following years of double-digit increases, the employees were exhausted from continuous rate increases and benefit reductions. They inherently knew that every dollar the company paid for their benefits was a dollar they didn't have for the bonus pool. However, employees directly felt the impact of the rate increases every year and it was amplified harder than any pay increase could offset it.

Saving the company money was good. Saving employees money was better. But finding a way to connect the program to improving and maintaining the health of the employees AND their families...to improve their quality of life and well-being WHILE they were saving money for those same loved ones became a far more compelling reason to start to change behavior.

Step 2: Build A Guiding Coalition

The transformation will be impossible to run as a one-person operation. If HR is trying to do this alone, it will fail. If the CEO is trying to implement this alone, it will fail. This effort MUST be a team effort led and managed by multiple people in the organization. Creating a team of supporters to help with the heavy lifting is essential. The first team following the executives from whom I gained support for the program is going to be the Wellness Committee.

The Wellness Committee is a group of representatives from throughout the organization. Whether this group has real authority is not essential – they have REAL influence. This group should reflect the interests and thoughts of everybody in the organization. It is this group that must be active in sharing their opinions, submitting their input, and becoming involved in the wellness programs throughout the company. As they become excited, they share their excitement with others and become the go-to people for all things related to wellness.

This approach generates a grassroots campaign that demonstrates support throughout the organization, spreads the workload, and creates an opportunity for others to be involved in growing and developing the program. It also provides a sounding board to share new ideas, closes the feedback loop to receive the feedback from them, and it creates goodwill as you launch new elements of your program.

Step 3: Form A Strategic Vision and Initiatives

As the ancient script says, "Where there is no vision, the people perish." This philosophy also works for your comprehensive shifts to wellness and benefits. Without an appropriate plan, and without a vision of knowing which way you are going to go, this becomes a challenging process.

It is essential that you know what you want from the program and the direction you're heading. That way, as you establish your initial goals, you can make progress towards the general direction. Then, as you more clearly define what you want out of your program, you can make sure that you head in the right direction.

Step 4: Enlist A Volunteer Army

In the case of wellness and benefits, the volunteer army is going to be your early adopters. Here's how the breakdown always goes:

25% of your employees will be excited early adopters driving the change

50% of your employees will follow the loudest voice

25% of your employees will resist the change no matter what happens

I have found this model to be accurate, no matter the change initiative. I joke that I can give away free money and the resistant 25% will complain that I don't give it away in the right denominations. In the case of my wellness program, which I will explain later, this is correct. I am giving away a lot of free money and they still won't do it.

The volunteer army in this case is my top 25% of early adopters. Getting them excited about the program and building momentum among that group is key to making this program work. As they become excited and participate in the programs, they will create the energy needed to motivate the middle 50% of your employees. They will also communicate the benefits of your program at the grassroots level. Understanding this perspective is essential for adoption in year two.

Step 5: Enable Action by Removing Barriers

Your program needs to be as easy as possible for participation. That doesn't mean that you need to give the farm away. I am a true believer that employees need to have "skin in the game" when it comes to rewards. Simply rewarding employees for participation doesn't necessarily work. Outcomes-based programs are far more effective when it comes to making the changes you are seeking when it comes to benefits and wellness programs. However, you will want to remove barriers to entry to the program. In other words, you want to make this as easy as possible to participate and remove every excuse for the employees to engage in action.

Step 6: Generate Short-Term Wins

Any time that you initiate a new program – especially something as massive as changes to benefits and wellness and something as personal as changes to lifestyle and behavior – you will need to demonstrate progress as soon as possible. When research into wellness program ROI first came out, they didn't want to overpromise and under deliver so they set an expectation of 3 to 5 years for an ROI. Let me say that any CFO or CEO who hears that they must wait for 3 to 5 years for an ROI on a program like this will not generate excitement. It wouldn't excite me either. That's a long time to wait. When we talk about the changes to behavior and lifestyle that are necessary to create the outcomes that are needed, there is no way that employees will wait 3 to 5 years to look for the benefits themselves.

Everybody wants to see the results now – we are all "instant gratification junkies". Let me share that I have not implemented these changes or this kind of a program without seeing an ROI within the first year. It's possible, but your ROI is dependent upon the level of investment that you make. At the risk of sounding cliché, there is massive "low hanging fruit" that you can take advantage of, create some quick short-term wins, promote those wins, and create the momentum in your program right away. As employees start to see the outcomes of their efforts, they will become excited very quickly and continue to work towards even bigger wins. Without creating these short-term wins right away and feeling the benefits of them, they will not generate the excitement necessary to continue to maintain the changes that will be necessary to support the change.

Step 7: Sustain Acceleration

As you gain momentum through the program launch, program rollout, and short-term wins, this is just the momentum generation. You will not achieve a peak by any means, but you will ramp up the program. It is necessary to generate momentum to create and sustain ACCELERATION. You cannot continue to accelerate forever, but you do need to implement the plan and accelerate gradually over time. As your employees learn more, understand more, and settle into the new way of life, they will come to know how it works and re-culture their behavior. In other words, they are figuring out how to create a new way of being. That takes time and SUSTAINED support and activity.

During the initial rollout, there needs to be considerable time, energy and support through the program administration. This step cannot merely be at the initiation of the program. It needs to be a spaced rollout through the first 1 to 2 years. The first few months will be a robust rollout, followed by the next few months of "feeding" information, incentives, activities, etc. as the program continues to be "fed" through the sustaining activities. As you roll into the second year, a few more programs will be added to enhance and support the first-year program. Once you turn the corner, you can settle in a little bit more, but you still must sustain the first year AND the second year as they continue to acclimate to the new way of being.

Sure, you will see changes and improvements immediately if you do this right. However, this sustained acceleration will go into the second year and possibly into the third year. I will share how this has worked in my experiences later in the book. Your plan must be a multiyear plan. You cannot do a "one and done" approach to implementing a comprehensive wellness program. It takes a supporting and sustaining process.

Step 8: Institute Change
As the steps fall into place, the change also happens. It's not to say that all seven steps need to be in place and completed before the change happens. The change will happen – it will happen gradually. As you go through each of the seven previous steps, you implement a little bit more and. Employees start to catch the vision and they begin to share their enthusiasm with others. Individuals make changes in their lives, they begin to save money like they never have before, and they share their story with a coworker. Another employee starts to go to the gym and lose weight and people ask, "what happened?" Another employee finds a new way to save hundreds of dollars on prescription drugs by using a service such as GoodRx and they start to spread the word to their coworkers.

Real and lasting change happens organically. Any time that an organization creates the "change of the month" approach, it is usually just a matter of time for employees to outlast it. Change that happens in a top-down approach where a massive change initiative is rolled out from the top without any input will create tremendous resistance… even if it is the best program ever created. By creating a program that rolls up a little bit slower, is built from the ground up, involves as many people as possible, and grows organically, you have a much better chance at sustained success that is lasting and works.

A Multi-Year Approach

I would love to tell you that you can go from zero-to-hero overnight on this. When you look back on your efforts in a while, it will seem like it was overnight. However, remember that it took you several years to create the current situation. You can't turn the giant ship on a dime. It's going to take time and continued effort to make this thing work. That said, it doesn't have to take a lot of years, but it will take a multi-year strategy to assist you in driving your vision to you where you want to go to make the changes necessary.

How long it takes depends on you, your investment, your support network, the number of people available to help, executive buy-in, funding, and the overall willingness of your employees to jump in. Consistent messaging is critical (even if you don't think it is constant) and ongoing efforts will help to ensure program success each step of the way.

There are several approaches that you can take to build in a "strategy". Your strategy may include restructuring of benefits programs, a move to self-funding, rollout of an HSA program, integration of a wellness program, or several other features. The strategy you come up with depends upon you, your priorities in your population. Regardless of the plan that you create, there are some things that you can implement sooner rather than later. In all cases you must take a multiyear approach when looking ahead at your timeline. From there, consider how to break out what is realistic to be able to accomplish over the next few years as you work towards that end goal.

Example: Integrated Wellness Program

Let's use wellness as an example.

I believe it is essential to tackle claims as the primary driver of your costs. The first way to address claims is to reduce them – and that comes from having healthy employees. An effective wellness program is so essential and core to any strategy that relates to controlling costs. Wellness programs typically are not known for an immediate ROI, so most CFOs are not super excited about hearing how wellness is a good thing (although I have yet to not have a positive ROI in the first year of my programs). The challenge generally doesn't come from the lack of ROI, but how we phrase it, pitch it and then report it after the fact.

Below is an idea of realistic expectations depending upon the level of commitment and investment you are willing to put in.

Year 0: The Sell

You're most likely going to have to pitch this idea and it will require change. Whether you are talking about bringing on a simple wellness program or a comprehensive integrated strategy, you must start somewhere, and this will take considerable conversation and work. It begins with an idea and you will need to create your guiding coalition from the ground up if you are going to make this work.

If you are like most organizations, you have two primary groups. Sometimes they overlap and you have individuals who belong to both groups. These groups include:

- **Decision-Makers**: These are the ones in critical positions that hold the authority to approve new programs and budgets you need to get the programs started. These are also the key players that will help to move forward with new initiatives, provide funding, approve changes to the policy, and other structural changes you will need to bring in new program designs that are at the institutional level.

- **Influencers**: Now and then you have influencers who are decision-makers. However, this group includes individuals to whom others in the organization respect. These are opinion leaders and the "been there, done that" crowd that are the true front-line leaders of the company. When individuals in this group speak, people listen...and this is the group you need to win over if you are going to successfully launch the program.

These conversations are a combination between the formal and the organic. You will need to have your initial plans in place about what you want, why you want it and how you plan to get it. The discussions with decision-makers may include a bit more formality with considerations of implementation cost, ROI, expected outcomes, and program impact. Your discussions with influencers will be far less formal than that...seeking to start conversations that will build momentum and support for what you are trying to accomplish. Your goal in this case is to influence the influencers.

The Year 0 plan does not involve a lot of PowerPoints and formal presentations when it comes to the population. Instead, it includes conversations, one-on-one discussions, and sharing of ideas about how things could be if they were different. For example, starting a conversation about what the world could be like if we skipped a year of increases to insurance, or if we offered employees a chance to save money if they didn't use all their insurance benefits, or offering employees cash and incentives to pass biometric standards that contributed to lower rates for everyone.

Identifying what matters most to your employee base – especially the interests of your decision-makers and influencers – and starting the conversation around "what if" can create a vision of how things *could* be. Before long, they will join in the conversation and eventually ask the question of "how" the program could work. From there, you can get them to ask the next question of how they can be part of the solution for your company. At that point, you have your next recruit for the Wellness Committee.

Strategies to Bend the Cost Curve

Year 1: Introduction

Successfully pitching your idea should result in (a) approval to launch a wellness program from the decision-makers and (b) the formation of a guiding coalition of supporters from among the employee base. With both elements of support in place, you're ready to begin.

Trying to go from "Zero" to a fully functioning plan overnight is a recipe for disaster. Like anything else, we need to learn to walk before we can run. The same goes for wellness and fully integrated plans that address behavior changes. That is not to say that you can't adopt some of this if your population isn't ready…it *is* to say that you need to be aware that your adoption of the program and schedule must be according to the needs, circumstances, and readiness that you work within.

I have found it best to use Year 1 as an opportunity to introduce wellness to the workplace. A full programmatic launch of your wellness program gives employees a whole year to heat the messages, voluntarily adopt the program, and become educated. This first full year becomes a year of "enculturation" wherein you can create your wellness message, brand, and presence that permeates the organization. The specific recipe for adoption will depend on you and your organization due to your unique nature and employee base. I have found the following elements to be essential ingredients to an effective program launch for the first year that sets a company up for success:

- **Wellness Committee**: I've addressed this group already and will continue to add more details later in the book. This group is the most critical you can assemble. By bringing together a representative group from your employee population, training them, and then handing the activity arm of your wellness program over to them (under your direction), it offloads a lot of work, increases engagement and improves the outcomes. The sooner you start up this committee, the sooner your life becomes more manageable. Many hands make light work.

- **Branding**: If there's one benefit to taking as many marketing classes as HR classes in my MBA program, it's knowing just how much marketing we do in HR. We market *all the time!!* If you can brand it, you can sell it. Brand your wellness program, make a logo, place it on your materials, t-shirts, swag and all your memos so you can create a brand identity and do it as soon as possible. As employees see your branding, it will legitimize your efforts ten-fold immediately and continue to solidify your efforts as you go. The better the logo, the better the validation. It works! Ask your marketing department.

- **Goals**: We spoke about your goals before and how to set them. My recommendation is to share them openly with your employees. Let them know what you (the company) are after AND what THEY can do to help you reach those goals. If they catch your vision and feel the purpose, they'll jump in to help. As you share your vision of the outcomes that they can benefit from (e.g., lower premiums, better health, higher profits), it won't take long for the buzz to catch on, at least with the early adopters.

- **Central Messaging**: Figure out what the central message is that you are trying to communicate and stick to the party lines. The primary messaging is like any other advertising that you do. Repetition brings conviction – it works for criminals, and it works for wellness. As you consistently share the same message, it will settle in and you will make believers out of your employees.

- **Education**: Along the way, be sure to educate your employees so they can become better consumers of healthcare. As they come to understand how healthcare works, their role in it, and how to make better choices, they will start making better choices. Many times, it is not a matter of not wanting to make better choices. It is instead a matter of not knowing how to make better choices. Once you start earning better tools in the tool kit, they have additional choices from which to select options for their healthcare.

- **Communication Strategy**: You may not have your complete communication strategy figured out during the first year. That is probably the case in any of these segments. However, come up with a sequence or a cadence that you want to follow initially as to what to communicate, how to communicate it, and its frequency. For example, you may create a basic newsletter and decide how often you will distribute it. Consider who will write it, how you will obtain contributions, and the types of messages you will send within the newsletter.

- **Activities**: It is essential to have an active and participative program when it comes to wellness. Incorporating activity is how engagement builds among employees. The more that you can gain interaction and involvement, the more likely it is to be successful. Wellness doesn't happen from a chair behind the desk. You need to get people up and moving - you need an engaging activity element. They don't have to do something every day, but you should be doing something regularly that involves people and let them have fun at work.

- **Engagement Platform**: To make this work, including some of the sophisticated features that I'll talk about later in the book, you need a platform that can help to track activities, points, incentives and other elements of your program. Ideally, this platform should be online and accessible to everybody through mobile devices and provide content to help them track activities, learn, engage, and support one another. For you, you need a system that can help track the details, incentives, and everything else that goes along with the program. Trust me – it won't be cheap, but it will be worth the price.

- **Swag**: Just like branding, if I have swag people become excited. You know how excited people are over T-shirts that are tossed out at a ballgame. Chances are good that the T-shirt doesn't even fit, and it probably has something on the front of it that you don't even like. In fact, the T-shirt is rolled up and you can't even see it but still we go crazy diving for a T-shirt. Imagine if we had the cool logo of your company's wellness program on the front of it. Imagine if you had water bottles or gym bags. The list can go on and on? People love swag…and if I have a brand connected with the swag, I can begin to create a presence that permeates the culture.

- **Incentives**: We will talk a bit more about incentives in the next section, but even during your first year you need to tie incentives and to the program. Even if they are small, there must be some tangibility to your plan. We have receptors that hardwire us for incentives that go beyond the trinkets and trash approach to rewards such as swag – this goes to cash, bigger prizes, and other incentives that make it worthwhile for employees. If you want to get people excited, offer something of substance as a part of becoming engaged or as a prize for the winners in some of your first wellness activities.

- **Wellness Fair**: If you do not do this already, I strongly recommend doing a wellness fair. Invite your vendors and other wellness-related businesses in to meet with your employees. Offer a ton of freebies, invite the spouses to stop by, and allow your employees to stop in and visit with your carriers, providers, and others in a relaxed and face-to-face environment. It's fun, it's cool, and it allows employees to have engagement with the vendors too.

Year 2: Integration

Provided that Year 1 went well and created the interest, involvement and initial results you had expected, Year 2 should allow you to integrate your wellness program into your benefits plan design. This step is where the "rubber meets the road" with your plan design and you can both (a) reward contributions for curbing costs and (b) allow non-contributors to pay a bit more for their lack of participation.

- **Plan Design Integration**: The best-case scenario is the ability to integrate wellness into the core benefit in a way that rewards individuals for directly contributing to bottom-line savings for the health plan. Providing incentives in the form of HSA contributions, premium discounts, and other positive types of direct contribution can help drive the desired behavior changes that you are seeking.

- **Lucrative Incentives**: Just identifying "incentives" is not enough. The incentives must be large enough to make them motivational. The employer must provide strong incentives to employees for helping to make a difference in the costs.

- **Onsite Biometrics**: Onsite biometrics are especially critical if part of the integrated services include incentives for biometric results. If you offer an incentive for biometric outcomes, it is essential to provide biometric testing services onsite.

- **Increased Activities:** The activities offered in Year 1 permit you to introduce wellness to the company. In Year 2, you should continue those activities and add more to them. By increasing the level of engagement, you can continue to expand to include other options that may be more enticing to people that may not otherwise be involved. As more people become involved and engaged, excitement will grow.

- **Expanded Support & Benefits**: While this first full year of integration will be a busy year, it is also an opportunity to look at other support mechanisms and perhaps other benefits that may be available to the program. If other side opportunities could help and support what you are trying to do, they may make sense to offer to the company at this time.

Year 3: Acclimation

With so much change in the first full year of integration (which shows up as Year 2 under this plan), it is not a bad idea to allow a second year of settling in to let employees acclimate to the new program. You do not have to keep everything the same. It is an excellent opportunity to add a few more program features to help enhance your offerings and their options to make the most of the new program that they just mastered during Year 2. Areas of emphasis during this second full year of integration may include:

- **Onsite Gym**: If you don't have one already, consider installing a gym on the premise. It may be a lot more affordable than you think. We installed one on-site during Year 0 with some of the cost savings that we had from a negotiation with the carriers. We ended up coming in way under budget with our renewals from what we had anticipated, and I took some of the cost savings to use for an on-site gym. The cost of remodeling a section of the basement and equipping it with commercial grade workout machines was under $100,000. When you put it in terms of the percentage of your total annual healthcare spend, my ROI was quick.

- **Onsite Personal Fitness Trainer**: If you have an on-site gym, it's even better if you have a personal trainer to assist with it. Because we had an on-site gym starting with Year 0, it had been around for a couple of years. We used some of the cost savings that we had seen during the first two years to begin paying for our trainer to come offer group classes in the afternoons. While this appears to be an expense, we are saving so much money from what we are doing (over a million per year in savings!) that we can afford to have the personal trainer there in the afternoons. The classes are full, personal success stories are abounding, and yes... I had them all sign waivers to avoid liability issues.

- **Individual Coaching**: We also offer one-on-one coaching at a couple of different levels. First, the on-site personal trainer also connects with about a dozen individuals who need some additional support for their success. These are cases with heavier weights, special needs, or who need extra help for personal health reasons. While I am not violating HIPAA by checking out each person's claims, it is not that hard to figure out what kind of physical ailments that each person may have. Spending some additional one-on-one coaching with the health coach, losing weight, adjusting nutritional habits, and getting the help they need will result in huge dividends over time. They have already shown huge rewards.

- **Weight Management Solutions**: There are several weight management solutions available to employers. I have tried solutions that involve sending wireless scales to the homes of employees synced to online coaches that help to monitor and connect with individuals to help them meet their physical goals. That had some success, but programs like this may find an apathetic reception after a few months of progress. In other cases, I have brought Weight Watchers onto the worksite and have even heavily subsidized them to provide support to employees and their meetings every week. Several other options are available to employers. By providing ongoing weight management solutions and trying out new approaches, you can demonstrate your commitment to supporting employees with their struggles.

- **Competitions and Engagement**: Never underestimate the value of good competition. It may seem like the same old thing, but if you keep the game fresh and create some new approaches to the competitions, it can continue to work for you. The challenge is to add a fresh approach now and then with new prizes and new twists to ensure a fresh perspective on engagement opportunities.

Year 4: Addiction

By the time you arrive in Year 4, the system should be flowing. That is not to say that all employees will be participating at the same level. You will still have a similar breakdown where about a quarter of your employees will be excited, engaged, and earn every point available for the program. Another 25% will be actively involved, but not hit the full participation. The third quarter of employees will do some of the steps, typically somewhat reluctant to their involvement, and the final group – the bottom quarter – will be kicking, screaming, and refusing. The lower groups are the same groups complaining about the high cost of healthcare and wonder what can be done about it while the upper groups continue to use their employer-paid benefits to take care of those costs.

Back to the top groups, you won't be able to take the program away at this point even if you want to. You should have the momentum built up and generating support and enthusiasm. However, it will not run itself nor will it succeed by itself. Ongoing program considerations must include the following to remain competitive and relevant:

- **Ongoing Activities**: It may go without saying, but people want to have fun. If your wellness program is boring, people will not participate. Even the most reluctant may not admit it, but they want to have fun. The program must be engaging. You cannot continue to have the same program over and over. You must continuously find new approaches to engage employees and find new ways to connect. All programs and activities are not going to be for everybody. You must find new opportunities to connect and never assume that you're going to find something that everybody will like.

- **Freshen Up the Wellness Committee**: If you have not had the opportunity to do so yet, now would be an excellent time to adjust your wellness committee. There may be some key individuals who you do not want to change because they are huge contributors. At the same time, they may be getting tired of being the go-to person every time you need a reliable volunteer. Finding an opportunity to bring in new blood, gain new perspectives, and to allow others to participate in the wellness committee is the chance to share leadership, spread the good word, and further engage others in the cause.

- **Continue to Purchase Swag**: Swag must be an ongoing line item in your budget. You need to keep it fresh and new. It must be interesting. Any time that we go to conferences now, it is not about finding swag for ourselves. It is about looking for new ideas to find swag that we can bring home and use for our program. Keep it fresh and fun.

- **Messaging that is Front and Center**: By this point in your program, it can be easy to become complacent. Even if the program is working well – especially if it is working well – it may be easy to forget how much communication is required to keep the momentum going. Be sure that your message is clear, the goals are consistent, and you are sharing the wins and the challenges along the way.

As mentioned, you may come across several other ideas that are necessary to be a part of your program. Heaven knows, this is only a very partial list of everything that we take into consideration or do as we consider the wellness program and all the steps it takes to make it effective. I mostly wanted to give you an idea of the different types of considerations to put down on paper as you begin the dialogue of sketching this out in a multiyear format.

A Multi-Constituent Approach

The best strategies take into consideration an approach that addresses the different needs of different members. Building a one-size-fits-all program will create a nothing-works-for-anyone outcome. Instead, consider your members and their situations as you design your plan in terms of care and incentives.

Much like our multiyear strategy, you must consider multiple constituents to ensure that your spending adequate time and energy where it makes sense to allocate it. You cannot please everyone and trying to do so is futile.

The principles of wellness follow very closely to the Pareto Principle (or the 80/20 rule) or 80% of your results come from focusing on the top 20% of contributors. We talk about the early adopters and the need to incorporate them into your plan as quickly and as much as possible. By doing so, they will have the most significant influence on the rest of the population. That follows as close to the Pareto principle is possible.

As a related corollary, 80% of your healthcare costs come from 20% of your members. Unfortunately, it is probably closer to 90/10 and in some cases, it may even be 95/5 as the breakout.

Let's consider some of the constituents who you are dealing with from different perspectives and the considerations that you may want to take as you build your program in your approach to managing it.

Care

- **Keeping the Healthiest Healthy**
  The most significant ROI for your program falls into this category. By keeping your healthy people healthy, you avoid high costs in the future - it's the smartest money you can spend. The adage that "an ounce of prevention is better than a pound of cure" applies to this group. It doesn't take much to keep this group on the straight and narrow path. They will also serve as

your greatest advocates, promoters and volunteers throughout the program.

Care for this group includes an investment in preventative services, health advocates, and wellness.

Time and again, the research indicates that our best efforts *should* be spent and directed here with this category. Unfortunately, we tend to ignore this group because they are...after all...healthy.

- **Improving Care for the Sickest**
  While I am not suggesting by any means that you "write off" your sick population – that's cold – I am suggesting that this group is your costliest group and falls primarily into a cost containment category. If trend and predictable patterns prevail, the likelihood that individuals in this group will significantly improve in condition, behavior or cost is low. This group is all about cost mitigation. The better you can improve quality and access to care to (a) reduce the need for future care, (b) eliminate the expansion for additional care, and (c) limit the cost of claims incurred by the condition, the more effective you can manage the claims.

- **Addressing the Middle**
  The middle 50% will generally go wherever the loudest voice goes. If you can capture the hearts and minds of the top contributors, they can generate the buzz that you are looking for to capture the interest and momentum of the middle group. If we don't do an excellent job of capturing the interest of the masses – not just capturing their attention now but capturing their interest – we could lose their interest early on and then it is much harder to attempt to capture it back later.

Adopters

- **Early Adopters**
  As you put together your programs, always keep in mind the role that early adopters play in those programs. Early adopters may be playing critical functions on the wellness committee or in

other positions. Consider what they would want or need as part of the program. Feel free to run new ideas past them as well. Using your early adopters as the focal point of developing and implementing new programs is not a bad idea. Eventually, everyone will become an adopter of the program, so gaining consensus from your early adopters is a good idea. They should be the ones who are willing to give you honest feedback about your new ideas.

- **Late Adopters**: Far too often, we manage by exception. We worry about how we are delivering a product or a service based upon the lowest common denominator. For example, are we concerned about sending an important message by text because 5% of our population doesn't check text messaging regularly? What we miss in that case is that 95% of our population DOES check their text messaging. We need to stop catering to the exception and focus on the majority if we are going to make a difference with the limited resources that we typically have.

- **Middle of the Road**: As mentioned before, roughly 50% of your employees who are in the "middle-of-the-road" group will follow the loudest voice. The key is to influence the positive early adopters and help them to gain the most booming positive voice for the middle group to follow. Building a program that is easily accessible and successful is a big help to ensure success with this group. Reducing barriers to entry is one of your most important steps to maximize participation.

Incentives

In all cases, the incentives must be large enough to motivate behavior change. Knowing what is at stake, it is essential to make appropriate investments in the incentives for the event, activity or the change that you're going to request. When building incentive programs, there are typically three groups to develop:

- **Rewards Junkies**: I called them this because they will do anything for points, water bottles, T-shirts, money, or whatever you are giving them. If you promise it, they will be after you for it. Once they receive it from you, they want the next thing. These individuals respond well to tangible rewards - it's a good group, but it is one that you must consistently feed with real incentives. Be sure to have plenty on hand and that you continuously update the rewards to keep them fresh.

- **Resistors**: You will always have resistors to your programs. Even if you set up the money in the hallway and were handing out free money, you would still have resistors to the program. The key in these cases is to identify what they are resisting, why they are opposing it, and then to find a way to work around that. If you can know before you set up the incentives program, you may have a shot creating a motivational incentive program for these individuals.

- **Middle of the Road**: When it comes to incentives, they must be motivational enough that an individual will change their behavior to obtain that reward. As I mentioned before, you cannot get million-dollar results with a five-dollar gift card. However, you *can* create small incremental changes for that same five-dollar gift card that may not generate the million-dollar outcomes today but depending upon the behavior that you are looking to change, it may result in that kind of cost savings over time.

PARTNERSHIPS

Strategies to Bend the Cost Curve

You Cannot Do This Alone

Taking on healthcare is a big deal. No matter the size of your team or the strength of your partnerships, there are going to be times when it feels like it's you against the world. You need as many people in your court as possible, and if you are genuinely on your own, this will never work. Your program's success does not depend upon how cool your swag is, how beautiful your logo is, or how much energy you can display at the company rally. Those are helpful to promote the program, but the real success will come with how much support you can gain from engagement at all levels. That engagement will require partnerships on multiple fronts.

You are going to be changing the culture within the organization. You are going to be asking your employees to change their behavior at the fundamental level. This change requires new actions for them and their families to produce results that they have never seen before. It will go to the core of the very fiber of your culture. To do that, it will take it a coordinated effort from all the players involved in your healthcare program.

You will find out very quickly just how many people "touch" your healthcare plan as you start into this. For our conversation, I'm going to break it into two groups: internal and external. The internal partnerships that I will consider are the major groups inside your employee base and their dependents. The external partnerships include those individuals and groups who affect your plan but are not directly employed or related to the program.

Internal Partnerships

You cannot create a revolution by keeping this information to yourself or by motivating you and your immediate team to act. Likewise, you don't have enough capacity to create and deploy this kind of a program on your own – not because you can't make it up on your own, but because you cannot successfully change the behavior of every single person in the workplace. It takes more than that to create the momentum and the motivation to generate the shift in behavior to create the lasting change necessary to make the needed change.

Let's consider the partnerships inside of the organization that are needed to make this work:

Guiding Coalition

When we described our new program in the context of change management, we did so following Kotter's 8-steps, which includes the creation of a guiding coalition. I shared the need to create the wellness committee as an element of that guiding coalition – and I will talk about them specifically in a moment – but other guiding coalitions should be considered.

You may consider those who have authority or influence in the organization as you identify participants of your guiding coalition. Anyone who has an opinion or is an influencer in the company whose opinions matter is someone you may want to consider including in your group of people with whom you discuss your ideas and strategies as you build and roll out a new program. In some cases, they may have time and capacity or even interest to take part in the new program. In other cases, it may just be a valuable opportunity to visit with them, share ideas, and gain their perspectives. At the very least, you can understand their views and feedback. You may even have them to begin to influence others as they do the work for you by sharing vital information throughout the organization.

Executive Team

It helps if you have the buy-in of the executive team to make this work. If they do not give you the buy-in that you need, you will not have the authority or internal credibility needed to create the momentum necessary for long-term success. So now comes the magic question:

How do you get it?

First, you must speak their language, which means you must stop talking in "HR-speak." If you go in talking about how it's going to make people feel, and it's good for the company, they will tell you, "That's nice." You need to DEMONSTRATE a crystal-clear ROI of how your program is going to either (a) save money or (b) make money for the company. It's that simple. What you are about to propose is going to require funding upfront to restructure benefits, restructure employee rewards, offer new incentives, create an administrative burden on individuals in the payroll and finance departments, and otherwise complicate people's lives. This approach will create whining that will reach the very top as you implement change. If you do not have a compelling argument as to why to do this and what it will do for the company within a reasonable period, it will not make them very excited.

Selling Wellness

When I talk about wellness with executives as a strategy to win cost challenge, these are the three primary objectives that I use as the bases for my arguments as a conversation starter:

- **Improve the health of employees and their families.**
  This step begins educating executives. If they don't know how healthcare works, they must to help work the problem. As we have said before, the number one driver of cost and healthcare is claims. The only REAL way to address healthcare costs is to reduce claims – and that means solving the problems, not the symptoms. Costs are ONLY symptoms, and if we continue only to address the costs, we never address the real problem. If we can reduce the number of claims by helping people become and stay healthy, then we can address the real issue. The bottom line is this: Healthy people don't need to go to the doctor as much, thus reducing our claims and reducing the costs associated with healthcare.

Secondary benefits to help your employees include under-

○ Lower Absenteeism - When employees aren't sick, they don't miss work. It seems to make sense, but research backs it up.

○ Fewer Accidents and Injuries - There is a strong correlation between healthier employees and improved safety results.

○ Lower Workers Compensation - Healthy employees benefit from better safety trends (as explained above) resulting in fewer workers compensation claims.

○ Higher Morale - Healthy employees are happy employees, and that directly impacts morale in the workplace.

○ Higher Productivity - Higher morale affects productivity and performance, and that affects the bottom line.

○ Improved Retention - When employees are healthy, happy, and enjoy where they work, they stay longer.

These are just a few of the benefits that come from improvements to your plan. Now, to gain the support of your C-Suite, add a price tag on to these. What would a 1% reduction in claims look like? Or a 5% reduction? You don't want to make promises you cannot keep, but you need to be able to translate these benefits into real numbers and projections.

- **Reduce the healthcare costs for employees and their families.** A second conversation starter addresses the total cost to families. Total compensation considers the overall increase to employees. A dollar saved in benefits is a dollar earned to the bottom line to the employee's household income. If we can save money on the benefit side, that is part of the equation for the company as we calculate total compensation. As we help employees figure out ways to save money on healthcare, it simultaneously helps them to increase their bottom line for their household income. As the company can contribute to their net worth, it improves on multiple fronts as we will discuss throughout this book.

- **Reduce the cost of healthcare expenditures for the company.**

If the first two points are being taken care of, this third point will happen by itself. If employees are healthier, claims will go down. If employees are saving money, the company will be saving money. In the end, the CEO and CFO primarily care about the company saving money. However, there is no way that you can gain the momentum and the support of your employees if all you care about is saving the company money. You will never win the support from the masses if that is your primary objective. By talking numbers and adding a dollar figure to each of your goals, you can demonstrate how one adds up to the other. By speaking in financial terms, it will become clear how each of these steps creates a substantial dollar valuation and directly impacts the bottom line.

With executive support, you can move forward with the programmatic backing. You will also need to ensure that the executives give you not only the financial support but also the word-of-mouth support, so they actively support the campaigns. It would be best if you receive their buy-in, so they show up to activities, participate in the events, and actively endorse what you are doing, knowing that it will help the bottom line and help them achieve their own goals in the end.

Trust me…they may do it on a leap of faith the first year. By the time they start to see the cost savings role in the second year, you won't need to sell them after that.

Wellness Committee

I've discussed the wellness committee in the past, but let's talk about a few more details regarding its purpose and composition.

The purpose of the wellness committee is to offload a lot of the heavy lifting when it comes to the programmatic side of this transformation. For those of you who suffer from control issues, this is where I am going to tell you to let it go. There are some parts of this program that you do need to control. There are other things, such as activities and events, that you need to let go of and let them run their course. If you want full engagement from employees, generating involvement from the wellness committee is the quickest way to make that happen.

The wellness committee allows employees from all around the company to become involved and feel as though they are owners of the program. I have typically used the wellness committee to drive the activity arm of the wellness program. I have asked the wellness committee to provide feedback to me from employees, give me the "word on the street," serve as points of contact throughout the company for any questions or concerns, and then give direction as to the types of activities that we do throughout the year. Activities such as weight loss competitions, walking competitions and events, summer Olympics, annual biometric screening events (in conjunction with our wellness incentives), yearly chili cookoff, monthly lunch and learn topics and speakers, sponsorships for team sports and outside events (e.g., area 5k runs), etc. are examples of activities for which the wellness committee steps in and takes over.

By handing these activities off to the wellness committee, they take ownership, gain commitment, create ongoing momentum, and maintain the grassroots level of participation for the program. They also maintain a certain level of evangelism for the program that spreads throughout the organization. It has created an organic leadership model that continues to run throughout the year. Every organization is different as to their approach to create their wellness committee, its membership, and composition. The important thing is to have a wellness committee that includes individuals from throughout your organization that meets regularly and is taking an active role in executing your program.

Employees
Employees must be a critical partner to your program for it to be successful. You must approach them as partners, explain to them that they are partners, and then treat them as partners. Most employers are happy to share the risk with employees when it comes time for cost increases. As costs increase, most employers share that cost increase with employees through increases to premiums, co-insurance, co-pays, deductibles, etc. Few if any are willing to pass along cost savings when they occur in the form of reductions to premiums, deductibles, co-pays, etc.

True partnerships mean that those partners share in BOTH the risks AND rewards. If you want to build greater trust, the company should take on a higher risk than the employees and share greater rewards with the employees than the company itself gains. We can talk about that a little later, but part of this partnership means committing to employees that they will gain as much as they will lose to the collaboration and then sticking to it. It may sound like an empty promise to employees if they have lost something in the past. That is why TRANSPARENCY is a MUST when it comes to this relationship.

No matter your approach, understand that three groups will emerge. I have shared this before, but let me recap those three groups:

- **Top 25%** - You will have the top 25% of early adopters who will become excited about the program, will adopt what you offer, and will try out anything that you provide. The key is to utilize these early adopters, reward them for helping you out, gaining their feedback in trust, and building rapport with them as soon as possible. Don't despair that you ONLY had 25% of early adoption. Be happy that you have 25% and move forward with them as your early adopter group. Let them be your guiding coalition and use them to gain feedback to tweak and adjust your program.

- **Middle 50%** - The middle 50% will go either way according to the loudest voice. If you will out the top 25% to be loud and excited, the middle 50% will go that way, following through with whichever compliance requirements exist because the top 25% said it was a good thing. However, if you do not grab hold of the top 25%, the bottom 25% will complain loud enough and take hold of the culture. That means that this middle group will lean towards the negativity and kill your program. This middle 50% will never be early adopters and will never be overly excited – you must control the sway of this middle group.

- **Bottom 25%** - No matter how good your program is or how logical it may sound...you will always have the bottom 25% that will be resistant to your change or program. I have said it before, and I will repeat it. You can give away free money, and they will still complain about it. Do not spend your time trying to sway the opinions or convince the bottom 25%. Instead, spend your time and energy reinforcing the top 25% and supporting the efforts of the middle 50%.

Spouses and Dependents

Don't forget about this group. When it comes to claims, spouses and dependents typically comprise at least 50% of your total cost. To only involve employees means that we are not only missing out on this large group, but the chances are good that we are missing out on several household decision-makers when it comes to healthcare and financial decisions.

Not to overly stereotype, but working in a male-dominated manufacturing environment, there are a few things that we know. First, if we send anything out by email, most people on the shop floor will not read it or pay attention to it. Second, if it is something important that affects the family, the information will probably not make it home even if they did read the email. Third, the wife is perhaps managing matters of healthcare and in many cases, the household finances. If information about managing healthcare and affecting finances never makes it home to the action takers and decision-makers, the behavior change will never take place. We had to come up with methods to ensure that the information made it home to the right people in a way that made sense and that supported the behavior change.

We took three approaches to make this happen. First, we designed our incentive program to include the spouses. Not only could the employee earn wellness incentives, but we also included the spouses who could earn wellness incentives through tobacco discounts and HSA contributions (deposited into the employees' HSA accounts). As the spouses found out that they could take an active role in helping earn money for the household, they became excited very quickly and started to learn more. Second, we started sending information directly to the homes during open enrollment time. This process included old-school mailers with booklets explaining the program, outlining details of our incentives, and explanations of how everything works. The intent was to send the information to the spouses so they could learn about the program and understand the mechanics of the incentives. Third, we invited the spouses to our information sessions at the workplace. While not all spouses came, the invitation created an atmosphere of openness to engage the spouses in the conversation. We also recorded the presentations and then made the links available to the spouses who could not make it. This combined approach increased engagement with the spouses and helped to engage the other half of the population, creating the claims.

Depending on your organization, you may have other players and partners with whom to form coalitions and relationships. The key is to identify who can help build and develop a program that works best for you and your company to move your program along.

External Partnerships

Like internal partnerships, there are several external partnerships upon which you must rely to ensure that you assemble the "dream team" for the success of your program. Because every company is different, your specific partners may vary. The following are partners with whom I have come to rely on the course of my experience.

Brokers

First, I love my broker's. I'm not afraid to come out and say that my primary brokers are Mercer. I have used them for years and will continue to do so. That's my unpaid and unrequested endorsement that comes after years of ongoing partnerships from multiple employment situations. My specific broker, Suzanne, has become an invaluable resource as we continuously try out new strategies to keep one step ahead of the continuously shifting healthcare horizon.

Now here's the issue… brokers are consultants, not magicians. Their job is not to do it for you. Their job is to provide advice, give you ideas, and bounce ideas off. Their job is NOT to do it for you. I say this because of one individual who approached their broker and asked them for solutions to take hold of the healthcare crisis that he was facing. He wondered if somebody they knew had done an excellent job. They referred him to spend some time with me and see what I was doing. After spending a couple of hours with me, I shared with him some of my strategies, but I clearly instructed him that HE needed to become educated, spend some time analyzing his plan, and go to work on his plan. Instead of heeding my instruction, he went back to the broker and shared that since he had been a client just like I was, he should have the same program that I had…but he didn't, and it was their fault… so he fired them as his broker. Um…that's not how it works. Ultimately this is YOUR plan.

It would help if you found the right broker. If your broker only comes to see you once-a-year about the time of renewals, they are not your brokers. They are pimping your insurance. Insurance happens year-round, so your broker should be working for you year-round. This process is a full-contact sport that requires ongoing strategies and work. You are paying a LOT of money to your brokers. They should be working FOR you. This approach is an active and engaging relationship where you do work, they do work, you have ideas, they have ideas, and you work together to come up with the right strategies that work for your company.

Now, that said, I do have two brokers. I have another insurance broker that is less conservative than Mercer. They come up with some great ideas that are less conventional and sometimes are just "out there." That gets my attention, and I like it. I use a couple of their services that are not available through Mercer. It creates a precise balance. It's great. Of course, it discombobulates the peaceful status quo of a healthy broker-client relationship, but in a Yin & Yang kind of way. That way, I always have fresh ideas coming to me that keep me on the cutting edge of new ideas and opportunities.

Carriers
Your insurance carriers need to be partners in this equation. They do not merely provide the insurance...your insurance package must match the needs of your employees. Your carriers must be willing to offer you a solution that is going to give a VALUE-ADDED approach to a plan that works for you. Any time that you take an off-the-shelf option and try to apply it to a diverse population, you're going to have challenges. This is especially the case when you try to cut corners and find a discount product and then pretend that it will serve the needs of your people.

Another challenge comes as you are held hostage by your carrier. Once you are in a plan, and you have no options to carve out your pharmacy or stop-loss solutions, you lose the flexibility to make the plan work in your favor. Once the carrier starts dictating the terms and conditions of your program, you have no flexibility. You must be in control of your solutions. It would help if you had a partner who understands your needs, your other partners' needs, and then played their part to facilitate the success of your goals.

Vendors
There is an array of vendor solutions that can help you facilitate your goals. Having created these programs in tiny HR departments, we do not have enough time to manage the solutions all day every day. We need vendor options that can become automated solutions and that talk to one another. This approach requires partnerships with vendors who genuinely become solution oriented and not strung up on their proprietary platforms in a way that they cannot allow others to interact with one another. Some

of our more effective vendors with whom we have worked are in areas such as the following topics.

- **Wellness**

  I am pretty sure that every time I go to an HR conference, the number of so-called "wellness" vendors has multiplied. What defines a "wellness" vendor is up to the imagination as it can mean just about anything as it pertains to employee wellness.

  Our most valuable assistance has come from the online platform that helps us to manage the program altogether. While we have used a one for the past few years to track participation, track points, and coordinate our rewards and incentives, there are several platforms out there. (In fact, the one we started seems to have outlived its usefulness...time to shop for one to meet our evolving needs.)

  What I appreciate about proactive wellness vendors are the ability to work with us to customize our program, communicate and coordinate with other vendors, and send that information to our incentive providers through the HSA platform. What that means for us is that I don't have to spend all day tracking points or managing incentives. As employees engage in their wellness activities, the system tracks participation. For example, they can link their fitness trackers (e.g., Fitbit, Garmin, and many others) to the online platform. As they meet their daily fitness goals, points track in the system for which they earn credit towards their HSA account. It's all automated, and I don't have to touch it.

  Having a partner like this reduces my administrative burden while increasing my capability to have a robust and comprehensive wellness strategy. The employees can be as engaged as they would like and in exchange, they can earn as many incentives as they choose up to the maximum contributions. This service is not cheap, but it is a lot less expensive, a lot more secure, a lot more streamlined and a lot more valuable than having a full-time employee take care of this ourselves.

- **HSA Providers**
A key reward mechanism to a comprehensive wellness program and benefits plan is the health savings account. Having a vendor that allows automated responses through the online wellness provider to send incentive reports to them, which trigger automatic payments to employees for contributions further enable us to automate the rewards program.

We use a company called American Benefits Group (ABG) primarily because of their ability to automate this process. They received the report from our online wellness platform which triggers an automatic deduction from our bank account to fund the wellness incentives, and those incentives are automatically deposited into individual HSA accounts each month based upon their activity as tracked in the online platform.

[Of course, the same company manages our Flexible Spending Accounts and our Health Reimbursement Accounts (for those individuals on the high deductible plan who are ineligible for the HSA).]

This partnership is another crucial element to our ability to automate an otherwise complex administrative component to the wellness program. To employees, the system works. On the administrative side, it could become very complicated if you try to manage this on your own. A partnership such as this is critical to make it all work.

- **Other Services**
As you continue to build your program, you will find others with whom you will build relationships that also help to serve your specific needs. For example, I have found the following to be essential partners at different times in my programs.

    o   Employee Assistance Programs - Offering additional assistance for mental health, emotional health, and other needs in the home front are essential to creating balance and support from a "total wellness" approach.

    o   Financial Wellness – We have rolled out several financial wellness programs to support a comprehensive approach. We have found that if employees can't take care of their finances, that affects physical health as well. We have been successful with programs like Smart Money (a Dave Ramsey program) and with resources offered through Charles Schwab (provided at no additional cost through our brokerage).

o   On-Site Fitness Trainer - I will provide additional details on this later, but we have found that providing on-site fitness services has been an essential component to remind people to live better.

Providers

A final group of partners with whom we develop a healthy relationship and working partnership is the providers – the doctors and institutions from whom employees receive care.

Many employers have moved to the concept of reference-based pricing as a solution to essentially strong-arm providers into a negotiated structure to deliver service at a given price. That approach may work well in smaller communities and with larger employers. I have not been in a situation where our company has had enough leverage to do something like that to make it worth the providers time. I can't say that I have enough expertise to tell you how to do it, so I won't pretend that I have expertise in reference-based pricing. Besides, I'm not a big fan of the potential risk that it places on employees when the bills become stuck "in the middle" between the employer and the doctor to get paid, and the employee finds himself or herself with collection letters coming because the company sat on the bill too long. Let's move on.

Here are some opportunities wherein I have had success concerning direct relationships with providers.

- **Independent Providers**
  In my efforts to find new solutions to high quality and lower cost healthcare, I came across a nearby hospital that was right in my backyard. This hospital was outside of the standard networks operating independently. Without an emergency room, it did not have the same negative overhead that most hospitals managed. It was operating efficiently and is run as a business. This approach

76

created new cost-saving opportunities for them and a different margin for negotiations.

As I began to have conversations with them, they offered me lower pricing. By working directly with them, I was able to arrange pricing that was less than their lowest published price for services. Paying them directly meant a reduction of their administrative burden to bill for services, a decrease of wait time, and significantly less hassle to facilitate the transaction.

To create the incentive for employees, I was able to offer those on the PPO plan free healthcare for going to this location. I could wave all deductibles, co-pays, and coinsurance immediately if they did their radiology or surgical procedures at this location. This discount would eliminate any costs for the employees by having the procedures or services done at this location. The employee wins by saving hundreds or thousands of dollars out of pocket, and the employer wins because the cost savings were worth thousands…even tens of thousands from what we would have paid in one of the network hospitals for the same procedures performed by the same doctors (yes, these are the same doctors that were practicing in the network hospitals).

For employees on the high deductible plans, the hospital would work with them to run the first-dollar amounts through the insurance until the employee met the deductible. Once reached, we waived the quantity remaining, still saving the employee hundreds or thousands of dollars out of pocket.

- **Medical Tourism**
  The concept of medical tourism – sending people to other locations for the same or better quality at the same or lower cost - it is not a new concept. However, not nearly enough people are taking advantage of the
  idea.

While we will go into detail on this a little later, I have two primary partnerships that have paid off tremendously.

The first partnership is with CIMA Hospital in Costa Rica. This hospital offers many of the same procedures that are available here in the United States, but at a cost savings of 60 to 70% after all travel costs. They are internationally accredited, follow the same practices and procedures as here in the United States, and their doctors are well trained – most of them having been trained here in the United States. I can send the employee and their travel companion to Costa Rica for the procedure. They can enjoy a brief medical vacation and return at no cost to them. Not only is the quality the same or better, but the net promoter score for CIMA Hospital is off the charts – typically in the mid-90%! In fact, I trusted it so much that I had surgery there myself.

The second partnership is through pharma tourism. We send people south of the border into Mexico for specialty drugs. We cover all their travel expenses, waive their co-pays and costs, and give them money on top of it. In the end, they save money, they make money, and the company saves money.

To help us in both cases, a medical concierge company called Medical Travel Option is there to assist us in making this work. Again, instead of trying to play travel agent along with everything else that my small department does, we can hand this off to somebody else to make it happen. This kind of partnership helps us to add one more piece to the otherwise potentially complex puzzle and make it happen.

Strategies to Bend the Cost Curve

STRATEGIES TO CONTROL THE CURVE

Take Control – How Employers Can Do Something

If you haven't figured out by now, the approach of this book is about taking action. I am a firm believer that there are plenty of people in this world who sit back to the side and say, "someone oughta do something about that." Everybody has an opinion about what "someone oughta"…and to make this program work; we must move from the group of "someone oughta's" to "I'm gonna." When you make that shift mentally, it affects what you can do physically. Organizationally, when you begin to believe that you actually CAN make a difference and do something about the healthcare crisis that you are in as a company, it affects your attitude, and you start to come up with solutions that you never saw before.

Moving from the status of "someone oughta" to "I'm gonna" provides a sense of freedom that invigorates and motivates. It allows you a new opportunity to engage at all levels and provide employees, executives, and other partners a chance to become part of the solution. In short:

It's never about IF, but HOW to make it happen…

This can-do mindset is critical to make the program work for you as the team leader as this will create the contagious nature of the vision that is needed to start the ball rolling.

With the "IF" question answered…and it needs to be a moot point by now (because the answer is "yes"), the next question of any employer who wants to take a shot at controlling the curve is this:

Do you believe you CAN control the curve?

Most employers want to do something about the curve, but don't know what the first step is. In other cases, they may believe they can control it, but only through negotiations with the carriers which typically results in minimal results if any.

Those who understand how healthcare works have the best chances of making it work in their favor. Understanding how it works and developing a relationship with the players within the system is essential to creating the influence necessary to effect that change.

It will take real leadership from companies to change the way they manage healthcare. Companies cannot sit back and expect their broker to come with the right solutions that will give them control over healthcare costs. This approach isn't because their broker isn't a good broker, or that they are not nice people, but because that is not how brokers work. Most brokers operate within the context of trying to save companies money within the confines of the game. YOU are going to need to be the one that comes up with the solution for YOUR company. Nobody is going to do it for you, and it won't come from a single source. This is going to be a learning process, and you're going to have to do your homework.

Coming up with your solution begins with creating a strategy. Your strategy is going to require an understanding of where you are starting from, a vision of what is possible, a realistic perspective of what you must work with, and knowledge of the tools in your toolkit. With this base, you can begin to formulate an action plan that makes sense. Let's start by analyzing where you are.

Continuous Improvement

Many corporate programs fail because we want them to be designed and laid out perfectly before we execute. When it comes to implementing your healthcare solution, you won't have the luxury to lay everything out before you perform. It's too complicated, it's too big, and it's too encompassing. Part of the challenge is that as you develop and evolve, some of the rules change. Not only do regulations and rules change along the way, but conditions change.

For example, as you start into your program, you may have a group of influencers or decision-makers who enjoy an aspect of your program. They may want more of something that you did not anticipate. You will need to pivot and offer more of a specific plan that takes you down a different path. In other cases, you may have a wellness platform that initially worked out well and was a core element to your plan. After a while, the vendor may no longer provide the same level of service to you, and you may need to pivot and find a different solution that does not offer the same answer as you had before. You may need to adjust the approach that you take.

Things may happen that are out of your control. So long as you have the vision and know where you want to go, you can keep going. The specifics of the program may vary along the way. Things happen. Shift happens, right? By having your vision laid out, regularly reviewing where you are going, and remaining flexible, you can begin the journey, bring people on board, and adjust as you go.

Continuous Improvement as the Tool
For the planners in the room who are unable to move past this notion of launching without a fully baked plan, let's give you a little bit of context and structure to make you feel better about doing it this way. I'm not saying to launch without a plan. I am saying to launch with a pretty good idea, a solid direction, and a process by which to follow so that you can adjust as you go.

Implementing a process such as continuous improvement may be part of that solution. For those starting from scratch, you still are not entirely starting from scratch. You have been doing something along the way when it comes to healthcare. The concepts and topics are not altogether foreign to you or your employees. You are taking something that you have done or are doing and improving upon it.

In some cases, these improvements and adjustments may appear radical. However, we are making improvements to something that is already known. We are improving upon something that exists.

Because we are taking something and improving upon it – in this case, healthcare – it's a matter of improvement. The human mind can wrap itself around something it already understands faster than something brand-new. Within that context, we can apply concepts of continuous *improvement* far more effectively than if we introduce this as something that is continuously *new*. Proposing this as a *better* approach to healthcare rather than a *new* approach to healthcare may help bring people on board a little faster and little more natural. It may also help them to come up with new ideas and strategies to *improve* the current process rather than resist a *new* program.

We can do this by implementing a more straightforward approach to process improvement. I tend to pour the Kool-Aid of shifting to the term "continuous improvement" because it's okay if you want to change or improve the process, but given the rate of change in business today, that change does need to be continuous as we review and revise it regularly. You are familiar with the terminology used with several improvement strategies that have been around for years, even decades. When you talk about concepts of lean, *kaizen*, Six Sigma, and other related ideas, you typically have a natural reaction of elation, exhaustion, despair, fear, or a home to the face ready for the next platitude. This reaction often comes from overuse of the terminology and not enough functionality or outcome.

Let me introduce a more straightforward approach that you can teach to anyone that applies to any situation. It may be part of the solution in this healthcare scenario.

In my book, *Doing HR Better*, I outline a simple four-step process to continuous improvement…

- **Identify** – Assess where you are to fully understand your starting point, whether it be good, bad, or indifferent. Within this step, you will also define your boundaries and constraints...how far you are willing and able to go to make your program a success.

- **Evaluate** – Take your assessment and evaluate it against where you *should* be. Consider what "good" looks like or what your desired end state is and determine the gap between where you are now and where you need to be. This difference is your gap analysis. This analysis will fundamentally serve as the Innovation Platform that we will use as the basis for planning and project management in the next step.

- **Plan** – Create a detailed plan on how to move from "here" to "there"...develop your action plan to move from where you are to your desired end state. Within this plan, you can develop the process wherein you can innovate your means to achieve repeatable successful outcomes.

- **Execute** – Now it's time to move into a state of what I refer to as "GSD"...Get Stuff Done. This change effort won't accomplish itself. It requires action, so identify your action items, prioritize your steps, and make the first moves. The changes won't be perfect, but we can experiment and refine as we go if it doesn't execute well the first time. Besides, ongoing refinement is part of the continuous improvement cycle that you must establish to build a *culture* of innovation.

Many managers are caught up in wanting to create the entire plan in detail before getting started. While I agree in principle that you should generally know what you want from your program, if you wait until you have every detail planned, you will never begin. You will fall prey to analysis paralysis. After you have a good idea of where to go and a decent structure to move with, it's time to act.

Step 1: Identify Where You Are

The initial assessment is essential to recognize your starting point fully. Assessing your situation may include the following elements:

- **Total Plan Cost and Trends**

It's good to know what your starting point is for the entire plan cost, but it is much better to understand what your trend has been for the past few years. For example, if you are a group of 500 employees, and your total cost per year is $6 million, is that good or bad? There are a lot of variables such as what is covered, your deductibles, plan design, number of high-cost claimants, etc. The better measure to know is what your trend has been for the past few years or past several years. Having a *relative* yardstick specific to you and your organization will be a far better measure than anything else you can use to determine progress as you move ahead with changes.

- **Employer/Employee Split**
  You may consider the current split between you and your employees. Affordability of healthcare is becoming a more significant factor in recruiting talent. In many cases, it is even more critical than wages. Recognizing where you stand with cost sharing and how you compared to the market will help you track your competitiveness and serve as a marker as you move forward to gain new levels of competitiveness as you make progress.

- **Utilization Rates**
  Knowing what your employees spend healthcare dollars on and how much they are spending are crucial to understanding how to improve your medical spend. Some things cannot be adjusted, such as prescriptions to specialty drugs that do not have generic equivalents. However, understanding how many emergency room visits take place during the middle of the day and for what conditions when urgent care centers are available for the same contingencies, can help you identify whether people are using the right facilities for the proper purposes. In some cases, a little bit of education can go a long way if you find that people are using the ER as their primary health care facility.

- **Population Overview and Demographics**
  Understanding your population is going to be vital to managing them. Are they old or young? Are they healthy or overweight? Are they single, married, or have large families? By understanding the makeup of your population, you can identify the best plan designs that will serve their needs, accommodate their conditions, maintain their health, and control costs in a way

that help me to meet your goals more effectively. Without an understanding of whom you are serving, there is a chance that you have the wrong plan design, and it could be costing you dearly.

- **Ability to Pay (Company)**
  When companies initially offered health insurance to employees in the past, they may have done so for several reasons such as benevolence, pressure, competitiveness, or something else. With the ongoing increases to the cost of healthcare, companies find themselves mitigating the costs through less than optimal solutions such as cost sharing and plan carve-outs. If the company's ability to pay is the primary basis for making decisions for plan design, this is important to understand upfront. In some cases, it is what it is. In other cases, however, the company executives may say that this is the primary driver when, in fact, they are only protecting cushy profits. We will talk about the value of investing in better plans for the long haul.

- **Ability to Pay (Employee)**
  A typical strategy in the past has been cost sharing. As costs have gone up, so to have been the portion of sharing those costs with employees in terms of premiums, deductibles, co-pays, out-of-pocket maximums, and other expenses. After years of cost sharing, employers are finding that they have reached a maximum point where they can no longer pass costs onto employees. They have hit a maximum point of cost sharing due to the affordability for employees.

Even if you have not hit this point yet, you may want to consider the employee's ability to pay as a factor for your plan goals and priorities. As this becomes a stated goal and is built into the core as one of your priorities - to make healthcare more affordable to your employees and to help save them money – that can bring them on board quickly. Then when you save a buck and pass savings on to them directly by lowering premiums and deductibles, having a premium holiday (skipping a payment on health insurance premiums around the Christmas holiday), or reducing costs at the point of service, employees start to catch on quickly about what they can do to help out.

Step 2: Evaluate Against Your Vision

In the next section, we are going to talk about your vision of where you want to be. By taking the time to assess where you are – truthfully, honestly, and objectively – you can clearly understand your starting point. If you do not take the time to perform an honest assessment, you will not have a firm foundation upon which you can build the rest of the program.

From here, consider what you want the program to be. You may not clearly understand all the details. That is common, especially if you have never done this before. Start with some goals or ideas of what you need out of the program. Identify what you need or what "good" looks like in significant areas of the program.

I recommend taking some time to do your homework. Consider your organization, its size, its industry, location, etc. Work with your broker to come up with trend analysis for your company and the industry. As you compare where you are to where you should be according to industry and company norms, this should give you a pretty good idea of how you compare to where you ought to be. If you were unclear before about where you should be, this base analysis should give you some ideas of areas upon which to work.

While each company is different and your specific outcomes will differ, you may consider the following topics to add as a minimum to loosely define and clarify your starting point for evaluative purposes:

- Employees

    o   What keeps you up at night when you think of your employees and their insurance coverage?

    o   What does "good" look like _to your employees_? (Feel free to ask a few or all of them.)

    o   What do you want for your employees as a result of your program?

- How will your employees' lives be better as a result of your program?

- What questions, concerns, or problem areas must your new program address that are not being met by your current benefits strategy?

- What are the most common sources of complaints from your current plan?

• Program

- In your "perfect world," what does your program look like?

- What must your program include?

- What must your program exclude?

- What do you need to include in the new program that does not exist in your current plan? Why?

- What are the elements you would like to have in the new program if possible? Why?

• Insurance Offering

- What are your "deal breakers"? (Those parts of the insurance plan that either must be in there or cannot be a part of the program…or the deal is off.)

- What are other companies offering that you are not?

- What are you offering that other companies do not? How much does that cost you?

• Savings

- How much do you need to save to make it worth your while?

o   How much do you <u>want</u> to save?

Based upon the industry analysis (your company analysis versus the industry analysis), you should come up with several other considerations and problem areas that pop out. This analysis is critical to conduct. Knowing what "good" looks like it is going to be essential for you to set your standards, identify standards against which you will measure your progress, and determined pivot points along the way. Without this, you will not know where adjustments are needed or how you are doing.

Step 3: Plan

Let's be honest. You will probably not have most of your plan thoroughly worked out before you launched. If this is your first time doing something like this, I guarantee you won't have most of it completed. However, it would help if you still had a game plan to lead you from where you are today to where you want to arrive. That is okay.

The plan must be a living document. I know that you hear that a lot when it comes to strategic planning. In this case, it must be a living document. This approach must be something that you refer to regularly and abide by as your operating plan. Without it, you're going to have challenges keeping all the balls in the air that will be flying around.

Your plan should have core elements included in it. We will discuss these in more detail in the following sections, but at a minimum, it should consist of strategic, funding, and programmatic content such as:

- Vision & Strategy

- Budget

- Structure

- Education

- Wellness

- Rewards

- Activities

Step 4: Execute

As Grandpa would say, "This plan won't work itself." It's great to analyze, prepare, and deliberate, but nothing will happen until we take our first step forward. Whether that first step is actual or symbolic (then followed by exact steps) doesn't matter...so long as action ensues, and things are done.

This approach also requires a new mindset - "GSD"... "Get Stuff Done!"

It comes in handy when you can tell your colleagues, spouse, and even yourself that you have to GSD the thing. It cuts to the chase and is crystal clear.

The thing about execution is that no matter how well we plan, something will generally not go 100% correctly. It happens. We need to allow for a threshold or a margin of error. If we involve others, we cannot only "take it back" if it doesn't go the way we wanted it to go when it is not in our hands. This is how learning takes place...and when it comes to changing behavior, there is a lot of "un-learning" of bad practices that must take place before new learning happens.

Remember...to FAIL refers to our First Attempt In Learning. If we take back everything all employees fail for the first time, it creates an unbearable load for us as managers, and we can never accomplish everything. Instead, we need to understand that execution is as much coaching and teaching as anything else. As we spend time developing others, we are teaching them to take the reins, to grow personally and professionally, and they expand their capabilities in what they do. Rather than a knee-jerk reaction at failure, the active manager recognizes failure as part of the learning process. So, the faster the employee can fail and learn from the experience, the faster the learning process generates higher performance.

As the employee achieves higher learning, followed by higher performance, the effective manager places the more top performers alongside developing employees to learn from the best. Staging learners

93

to gain experience, learn exponentially, then share that knowledge with others on routine procedures improves the learning process and enhances retention exponentially.

When it comes to the wellness plan, you will try some things out that work and that don't work. As things work, evaluate what made them successful so you can continue to use it in the future. As they don't work, learn from it, apply for the future, and try again later.

Your Vision & Strategy

We've talked about your vision for the future - an image of what you want as a result of the program. It's worth spending a bit more time understanding where you want to go with your plan before you begin the journey. Without a clear understanding of where to go, you may spend an inordinate amount of time trying to figure out what to do, where to go, and how to do it.

Let's spend some time clarifying your vision of the desired outcome before we build your To-Do List.

Initial Assessment: Starting Point

To understand where you can go, it is essential to know where you are. We must understand claims, trends, and data relative to your population. It also includes an analytical conversation asking "what if" questions to determine what the future might hold under different realities.

I recommend a deep dive into your data analytics. You should expect one of three options depending on your experience and situation:

- **Fully Funded**: With fully funded plans, you are at the mercy of the carrier to provide you with data. If you have a good consultant with deep analytical tools, you may be able to receive a better analysis of your trends. I wouldn't hold my breath. Understandably, different carriers have different perspectives on the transparency of data. The data is theirs, and they will decide what information you are able to see. Still, take the data that you can and analyze the heck out of it.

- **Self-Insured – Limited Data**: Most self-insured groups still rely upon carrier data for their primary source of information. They receive the annual reports, trend reports, and perhaps some additional information through their brokers. You may have access to other data because the data is now yours – not theirs. Check with your broker to see if you have access to additional analytical tools through them for improved analysis.

95

- **Self-Insured – Expanded Data**: Employers who understand the need for independence in data analysis will contract with an independent third-party such as NavMD to run the data. For example, I use them to tap into the data from my carriers, correlate it, extrapolate it, run the trends, identify correlations, and evaluate the results. A third-party can create "information" for my review and not just prepare more data.

Back to my previous point, I can't fix what I don't know. By running a deep dive into my data, I can figure out where my problem areas are and build a solution around addressing them. Part of my vision, then, is to provide specific resources to help individuals in those categories in a way that helps to improve their health, well-being, and wallet.

Additional Considerations

As part of your initial assessment, you may also want to consider a few qualitative considerations.

- **What are my pain points?**
  Identify the key drivers that cause you the most problems, significant challenges, highest costs, most time, greatest frustrations, etc. Those are the most significant pain points to address through any program that you undertake.

- **What if we do nothing?**
  As an analysis, you must consider what would happen if you did nothing. There may be some benefits in terms of a sense of comfort with sticking with the status quo. However, you will never be able to improve anything if you keep doing what you've always been doing. Remember the definition of "insanity"? (Doing what you've always been doing and expecting different results.)

- **What is important to employees?**
  Consider what employees complain about the most, such as cost, access, coverage, service, or something else. List out what they express you are their most significant concerns. If you are not sure, this and some of the other questions that you identify here may be the subject of a survey to conduct.

- **What are the minimums that need to exist?**
  With any program, you need to understand what your minimums are. There are some requirements that you must have no matter what. It may sound simplistic or that some things are simply a given. It is essential to identify what they are so that you can keep that in mind. As you construct your program, consider what matters most, and place it at the forefront.

- **What CAN I do?**
  This question assesses your current sense of reality. Here you start to identify what you think you can do right now. I guarantee that as you begin this process, you're going to feel limited and disempowered. As you continue through this exercise, you will identify some opportunities that you didn't have before, and this list will change.

- **What COULD I do?**
  This question should take you to a different level. This question is what you could do if you had the power to do it. What changes could you make that could change the lives of your employees? If you could change anything about the plan and program today that would have the most significant impact on your employees for good, what would it be? List that out. It doesn't matter if it takes people out of their comfort zone. List it out. What you will find is that you will be able to accomplish more than you think you can today.

- **What MUST I do?**
  During the initial assessment, you may not know what falls into this "must" category. As you continue with your evaluation, it may become apparent what needs to be done for change to happen.

Budget

Initially, you will need to identify a budget that is available for your project. This budget will be at the core of your success each year so you must keep track of it each year and update it meticulously. I find the need to budget precisely for my program each year to support the program outcomes. Just like any other investment, it takes money to make money...wellness and programmatic changes are not free. You may have different needs and specifics, but the following are some of my more prominent categories of spending that I budget for:

- **HSA Contributions**
  As part of my program, wellness contributions through the health savings account represent by far the most significant investment each year that we make as an employer.

- **Gym Equipment & Maintenance**
  I mentioned that we set up the gym in Year 0. Keep in mind that it will require maintenance, repair, cleaning, upkeep, depreciation, and replacement every year.

- **Online Platform**
  Given the small team that I have, it is essential to have an online platform to track participation, rewards, points, etc. It also helps with HIPPA compliance to reduce the amount of exposure that I have to personal health information. Anything that can help me to automate processes and reduce exposure to liability is a huge help. Then when I can facilitate access to employees, improve functionality, and make it fun, this is worth every dollar. These online wellness platforms are not inexpensive.

- **Rewards**
  Related to the online platform are rewards. As people accumulate points, they can typically cash in these points for things such as gift cards or merchandise. Somebody must pay for it – and that is you the employer. I need to budget for those rewards as a part of the online platform. That is also not a modest amount. However, it does drive engagement and is a vital part of the program.

- **Swag**
  Just like any other marketing campaign, promotional materials are a crucial part of your wellness program. T-shirts, water bottles, gym bags, and other swag items are essential to keep people motivated and engaged. It creates a visual impact and maintains the program in front of them. Just like branding, this helps you to preserve the message of health and well-being for your employees.

- **Activities**
  Of all the things that I budget for, the activity component of wellness is the least expensive of all of them. The wellness committee typically organizes and runs the activities and events. Still, some activities cost money. For example:

  - Sponsorship of the company softball team
  - Support of teams for the corporate fun run
  - Uniforms or T-shirts for teams in local sporting events
  - Materials costs for activities
  - Food costs for activities
  - Speaker fees for lunch and learns

- **On-Site Trainer**
  Our on-site trainer in the gym does not work for free. She costs about as much as a regular trainer would. I need to budget for that.

- **Onsite Biometrics and Testing**
  To bring biometric screening on-site will cost money. To reduce and eliminate barriers to participation, we make biometric testing free. The testing will cost money, so include it in the budget.

Sources of Revenue

Only listing the source of the cost will become a depressing exercise if you do not understand where the sources of revenue are to generate some of the funds to offset those costs. The first year of implementation will be a cost-only proposal because you won't likely have a source of revenue related to the program. As you begin to see the benefits of the program, additional sources of funding will start to emerge. Consider the following:

- **Tobacco Premiums**
  Whether you charge a premium for tobacco use or you offer a "discount" for those who do not use tobacco, there is a difference in what people pay for their premiums between those who use tobacco and those who do not use tobacco. (Keep in mind that I am an advocate for using cotinine screening rather than simply trusting the word of honor when you have a substantial tobacco discount.) Consider using the money that you collect from this differential to help offset some of your costs.

- **Wellness Premiums**
  If you do not offer HSA or similar wellness incentives, but you may offer discounts to premiums for jumping through some wellness hoops, that may be some additional money that you have access to that can help to offset some of your costs.

- **Premium Differentials**
  If you offer two different types of plans that may be designated by high deductible versus PPO, wellness based, or some other kind of factor, you may consider using the differential between the cost of the two plans as the basis for covering some of your expenses.

- **Cost Savings/Reserves**
  Perhaps the simplest way to do it is to run everything through a single account where you keep your cash reserves from the plan. Yes, you want to have your cash reserves tucked away if you are self-insured. You want to maintain that minimum balance to cover what needs to be covered. However, if you build up a cash reserve that is large enough and stable enough, that may also work out well as the primary source of funding for some of these costs to run through so as you build up the reserve you can help to offset your costs directly.

Structure & Plan Designs

Your next consideration to help control costs is your plan structure and plan design. We start with the great debates of self-funding versus fully funding your plan and then move into the plan design elements of high-deductible programs and HSAs to support them.

Self-Funded vs. Fully Funded

Many wonder if these ideas are possible when they are in a fully funded program. The answer is "YES"! The first time I guided a fundamental mind shift that saved millions was in a fully funded environment. To take it a step further, it was public sector and in higher education. After just the first year in that first "experiment" over 12 years ago, we could show demonstrable results that saved the organization almost a million dollars the first year in claims resulting in significantly reduced renewals, followed by three years of 0% or 1% rate increases. Compared to the several years of renewals before that, the wellness program can take credit - and that program is still in place today (they just went self-funded this year).

That's not to say that every program that we introduce in this book can work in a fully funded program. However, being fully funded is not a reason to ignore these ideas.

Many will say that they are not sure if they can "afford" to move over to a self-insured model. I understand several companies have cash flow challenges and may not be able to absorb fluctuations in a given year. However, when you think about it, *you're going to pay for the cost increase!!* It's a matter of whether you pay for it all at once (self-funded) or continue to pay for it over and over year after year (fully funded).

The value of self-funding is that you receive an immediate return when times are good. You do feel the pain when times are tough – and you will have a challenging year. However, you can also build your reserves up to absorb some or all that shock without having to feel the pain. That's just smart business.

High Deductible Plans

Most employers look to high deductible plans as a saving grace to make their programs work. Employers may see it as the way to build in affordability to the plan and opportunity for employees to save money. In theory, this makes sense – if employees stay healthy, they don't go to the doctor, they don't spend money, and instead they can save their money in the HSA over time and effectively create a 401(k) for future healthcare needs. Unfortunately, employers have been taking advantage of the high deductible plans, and they have not been practical tools to help bring down costs over the long term mainly due to:

- **Excessively High Deductibles**: The point of a high deductible plan is to put more responsibility on the individual to be a better consumer of healthcare. As they put money to the side, make better choices, and save money, they can benefit from those cost savings as well. When an employer puts a nominal deductible in place, this creates a point of entry that is reasonable to the employee, and people can make this work. When the deductible is almost the same as the out-of-pocket maximum of $6,600, it almost becomes unreasonable to expect the employees to become excited about the opportunities to save money under this kind of a plan.

- **Continuous Increases to Premiums**: Despite the promise of lower healthcare costs, individuals on the high deductible plans may be receiving the same rates of premium increases as those on traditional PPO plans. It doesn't make as much sense for those individuals to remain on the high deductible plan after all if they cannot perceive an immediate or obvious incentive for the higher risk.

- **Not Enough Incentives**: When an employer offers a high deductible plan with a very high deductible, but then believes it is doing the employee a favor by offering to fund the HSA with a contribution of $500, it is not doing any favors at all. It is adding insult to injury. The secret to making this entire thing work is to have employees to start acting like partners – like educated consumers. If they do not have the capital to make the proper decisions and purchase accordingly, they will never be able to make it work.

I have found that high deductible plans are essential to make the program work. However, they must function in a way that is congruent with your goals and objectives. They must include the following characteristics:

- **Accessible Premium**: First, the premium for the high deductible plan must be so attractive compared to the other option(s) that it will make no sense to go the other way. If you offer a PPO with your high deductible plan, the employee rate for the high deductible plan must be so evident that it catches the employees' attention immediately. You must make the difference in rates substantial. In plain English, it must be substantially less expensive and more attractive to jump into something new than to stick with the easy PPO plan.

- **Accessible Deductible**: Second, the deductible must be affordable. From my perspective, if you are starting with a high deductible plan, it's going to be a shock if you're coming off a standard PPO plan. Our intent is to shift them in the habit of doing something new, so we needed to make it as easy as possible. I decided to go with a point-of-entry that was as low as possible that still qualified for HSA participation. I decided to go with a deductible that was as low as possible – the lowest possible deductible for federal law. This approach saves the plan money, allowed employees to begin the process, and created the mechanism for me to create the program.

- **Funding Mechanism**: I will address this next, but to make this work, you will need to have a mechanism that allows employees to fund their high deductible plan. Sure, we can all dream that they will all set aside enough money themselves in a pretax savings account to cover their costs. Realistically, this won't happen. You will need to create a mechanism as an employer to provide them with incentives that will help to fund the cost of healthcare. In other words, the secret to this entire thing is to give the money back. Trust me; I've done this more than once – this IS the secret of making this whole program work.

- **Education**: We often fall into the mode of "this just makes sense." So, if it makes sense to us, it should make sense to everyone. It's easy to do; however, we cannot make that assumption. It is essential to educate – a lot. Repetition brings

103

conviction. The more you do the math and show them how it works, the more they will catch on.

Funding Mechanisms – HSAs

Let's talk about the funding mechanism to make your plan work. Once you set up your high-deductible plan, you provide the structural foundation upon which you can build a platform for lower costs. Effectively, you have shifted the "first-dollar" costs over to the employee. Now, what will you do with that money that you were once paying into the plan? You have a few choices. You can take the money and "run"…go use it somewhere else in the business and call it a win. However, this is a one-time deal. Once you save that money, it's gone. You'll never receive it back and you'll forget about it next year.

Another option is to avoid the temptation and instead re-invest those funds back into the program perpetually. The best ROI can come by taking the money that you save and **giving it back to employees**. Stay with me because this is where the magic comes from the entire plan.

Several companies "seed" the HSA by making a deposit. As a token "thank you" for choosing the HSA over the PPO, they contribute to getting employees started. If the deductible is high and the contribution is low (say, a $4,000 deductible with a $500 contribution), the gesture almost becomes insulting. However, seeding the plan gives employees money. Good, bad or indifferent, they have the money, and they are not encouraged or motivated to use it differently than they had before. They have "some" skin in the game.

In a few cases, I have seen the employer fund most of the deductible the first year (e.g., $2,000 of the $2,500 deductible in year 1 to get it started) with the motivation for the employee to set aside enough money to make it work from there. That's generous, but it does not provide the means to afford the costs when you are in the second year. Imagine an employee with five kids trying to pay the mortgage and feed the kids, facing a $2,500 deductible per family member multiplied by the family deductible where they must meet three deductibles. That's a lot of money to pay before the benefit becomes a benefit.

When you provide employees with an accessible option in pricing, a reasonable deductible, and the opportunity to earn most or all the deductible through an outcomes-based and participatory-based program, you can engage your workforce to become part of the solution. When you offer incentives large enough to motivate behavior change, you can influence change.

Employee Education

An essential part of your partnership with employees is to make them educated consumers of healthcare. What you understand to be the "basics" may still be a foreign language to most of your employees. They may struggle with basic concepts of deductibles and copays or think that the ER is a great place to go for a sprained ankle on a Saturday afternoon even though the Urgent Care is right next door.

Educating employees is one of the fastest and effective ways to build your program and start to make a difference. Here are some principles to begin with:

- **Insurance is Insurance**: I've said it multiple times and will continue to say it. When employees understand that health insurance works the same as car insurance, they will start to catch on to how it all works and will immediately become better consumers of healthcare. The reason we don't speed is that when we receive a speeding ticket, our insurance rates go up for demonstrating higher risk. Likewise, when we wreck our car and fix it, our prices go up.

  When we wreck our bodies, and we take it in to get "fixed" through surgery and expensive treatments, it generates claims. Those claims drive up costs. These conditions also increase the risks which drive up overall risk factors, thereby raising total projected costs (fully funded) or actual costs (self-funded). Either way, if we have high-risk members or individuals with high-cost claims, it drives up prices.

  When employees understand that their behaviors DIRECTLY impact claims (which then impact premiums), they start to pitch in to be part of the solution.

- **Educating Spouses**: Most employers focus on sending information to the employees and forget that spouses incur half (or more) of the overall claims. Without involving spouses in education and the solution, you cannot create the full partnership that it will take to make a difference.

I found this to especially influence workspaces with a male-heavy work environment like manufacturing. We could share information all day long, but let's be honest. The guys were not that great at bringing information home to their wives, and they are the ones who did most of the management of healthcare, finances, trips to the doctor with the kids, etc. If we did not educate the spouses, we were missing the opportunity to inform the primary decision-makers for the entire program.

We'll talk about specific strategies in a bit, but we took a multi-strategy approach to communicate with both the employee and the spouse to ensure that we connected with everyone. We communicated by email of course, but we also sent mailers home via US mail to be sure that it arrived. That alone was the #1 method to ensure successful communication and education of critical program information and changes. We also held group sessions and invited spouses to attend, onsite wellness fairs that spouses could attend, and onsite consultations with employees and spouses to answer any questions. As spouses became educated, they learned of ways that they could save money, which also helped the plan save money.

- **Managing Dependents**: While the Affordable Care Act has provided new assistance to many, it has also presented new challenges for employers. Keeping kids on until age 26 has created challenges for tracking dependents. It has also created challenges to keep the older kids educated about how to maintain personal health, make good healthcare choices, and how to avoid driving up costs.

Some common challenges come when they are at college away from mom and dad. When they are sick, they don't go to the doctor until it's too late. Instead of treating the illness early (and inexpensively), they wait until they have pneumonia (often resulting in expensive treatment and hospitalization). Another common challenge is using the Emergency Room as the primary care option rather than finding a doctor or using something less expensive, such as Urgent Care or telemedicine. Educating parents and older dependents on ways to reduce costs can save the plan thousands a year while improving overall health and wellbeing of all family members.

- **Quantity OVER Quality**: When it comes to education, some employers fall into analysis paralysis…waiting to perfect that internal marketing piece before they send it out. It's nice for it to look professional, but it's more important to send it out. Sharing information, having healthcare in front of employees, having honest conversations, and sharing best practices to help them save money are critical strategies for this to work.

  That is not to say that you shouldn't have aesthetically pleasing collateral to send to employees. You gain professional credibility in your program through the look and appearance of what you send out. However, every message you send out does not need to look like it came out of the marketing department.

  Open communication, continuous messaging, and ongoing updates are vital to keeping your program in front of your employees. Remember – this is the second largest expenditure on your books, so managing it is a YEAR-ROUND process, and your communication strategy must be year-round to help employees manage their healthcare.

- **Just Do It**: Finally, start somewhere. It would be great to have a comprehensive healthcare strategy fully developed and in a nice binder ready to distribute to upper management. Most of us are running on a skeleton crew to handle healthcare along with everything else. If you wait until every detail is planned out, you'll never start this. Communication needs to happen – to figure out how to begin and start somewhere.

Your Education Strategy

Educating your employee partners is essential to make the changes happen and to maintain those changes over time. I have found the following elements to be critical to the employee education strategy to remain effective over time.

- **Program Goals**
  Your program goals must be communicated consistently and continuously throughout your educational process. For

employees to believe what you say, they need to hear it, and they need to believe it. Your goals must be convincing, and they must have a meaningful impact.

Provided that you have set goals that are relevant, meaningful, and embraced by your employees, this will be at the heart of your change process. When my employees consistently hear that our goals are (in rank order):

o   To improve and maintain the health and well-being of employees and their families.

o   To reduce the cost of healthcare for employees and their families.

o   To reduce the cost of healthcare for the company (thereby improving profitability, which enhances the bonus pool and profit-sharing programs).

…they can start to buy into it.

Then when I return and report our progress in terms of metrics and reminders followed by program results in the form of cost reduction measures that affect premiums, co-pays, and other out-of-pocket costs, it earns their attention.

• **Consistent Messaging**
  Just like any other messaging, you must send a consistent message. You can change the priorities periodically depending upon what your focus is. Each year, depending upon what the data say, we may have different sub-priorities or new programs that we roll out. For example, we may introduce a new coaching program or a new diabetic management program to help support our goals.

However, we consistently focus on improvements to personal health and well-being, individual choice in consumerism that reduce costs to the plan, individual wellness efforts for long-term success, and the rewards that come from making good choices. Over just a short time, this has become part of the culture.

- **Communication Channels**
  We have found that an effective education process requires the use of multiple channels. With a diverse group of employees, not everybody receives information in the same way. Sure, everybody has an email account. However, that doesn't mean that everybody reads their email or that even if they did, they would receive the same meaning.

  A multichannel approach considers your audience and the best ways to reach them what the messages that you are trying to send. In our case, we have not only the employees but also their spouses and dependents who affect the claims which drive costs. We recognize the need to communicate digitally with younger employees, in hard copy format with more seasoned employees, by traditional mail to dependents to ensure that they receive communication at home, by video (via YouTube) to communicate longer pieces of information such as open-enrollment videos and other strategies.

  The better we can communicate with all the constituents, the better we can deliver more information. The better we can increase understanding, the better we can create shared meaning. As we create a shared purpose, we can all work towards the same goals.

- **Frequency**
  Effective education strategies require the ongoing transmittal of information to refresh, enhance, and engage. One-time educational processes do not work. Even if the information is received the first time, learning drops over time. With so many moving parts to a sophisticated wellness program, it is easy for an individual to forget essential information or only to pay attention to certain parts at certain times. Forgetting may be fine now, but it may be costly to them or the company if they do not pay attention to critical elements of the strategy over time.

  Spaced learning is a practical approach to training and development that takes place as bits and pieces of education happen over time. This approach to learning also allows the learner to receive a part of the information, digest it, apply it, and then move onto the next. The same applies to education when it comes to wellness and consumerism. While a tremendous amount of information is necessary at the start of the program, we have found it to be useful to use this trickle spaced learning approach to introduce new information and educate employees on these topics.

- **Visual Imagery**
  I hear several people in HR tell me that "function over form" is more important. I beg to differ. People do not want to read something that is ugly or appears to be challenging to understand. Since we have talked a bit about what "good" looks like, let's spend some time talking about what "ugly" looks like when it comes to your educational materials.

  o Poorly laid out materials would be a turnoff – if you thought they would not read your materials before, try sending out your new program outline in a poorly constructed form. Instead, use a nicely laid out approach following sound principles of graphic design. Use the in-house designer – most of you have one – to provide recommendations, structure, and perhaps even offer a template to follow that can help.

  o Follow a standard color guide that makes sense. Using clashing colors is an immediate turnoff while congruent colors can help to stimulate the visual senses and connect meaning to the imagery.

  o Consider the flow of information. Does it make sense contextually? Chronologically? Spend some time away from the content and come back to see how it looks and feels. Be sure to ask others to look at it as well and solicit feedback from all types...not just those with whom you work with each day.

To summarize, if your materials look "homemade," they won't fly. The more professional your promotional materials, the greater the legitimacy you will enjoy. Spend a bit of time ramping up the look and feel of your documents to move past the initial bias that comes in the first few seconds of exposure and make it easy for your employees to recognize the central message and meaning to your materials quickly.

Wellness: Selling the Benefits

When I arrive to this point in my conversation about changes to health care, several people have told me that they have "Been there, done that." After all, nearly 90% of employers offer incentives to employees who work towards becoming healthier. They also told me that wellness doesn't work, that it's too soft, and that it cannot generate the changes that are necessary to save the money that they are talking about needing to save to make benefits work.

It doesn't take long for me to ask a question or two to find out just how invested they were in their wellness activities to determine that they did not spend nearly as much time, energy or money into wellness as they needed to. They took some token efforts to dip their toes in wellness and then complained about it not working. *They wanted a disproportionate return on their investment.* That is not how it works. Wellness, like anything else, requires an investment – and your wellness ROI is in direct proportion to the investment of time, energy, and money that you invest in the program.

If you want any of these strategies to work over time, wellness MUST be part of your long-term strategy. The only real solution to reducing costs is to minimize claims and thereby reduce the need to go into the doctor or hospital in the first place. It's a simple fact that healthy people are sick less and impact the claims significantly less (or not at all). This step is really at the core of our overall goal.

There are so many vendors peddling wellness in so many ways that it becomes challenging to understand what true wellness entails. Let me break it down into simple terms.

First, when an employee is not sick, injured, or debilitated, he/she doesn't need to go to the doctor for treatment. When they don't go see the doctor, they don't incur claims…which in turn, don't drive up healthcare costs. Period.

Too simplistic? It may seem like it. Yes, bad things happen to good people. Accidents happen. Cancer comes. Genetics create dispositions to certain conditions. However, those are NOT what is driving most healthcare costs. Right now, 75-85 cents of every dollar spent on healthcare is for something related to a condition that most likely could have been positively affected by exercise, nutrition, or lifestyle accommodations. Wouldn't it make sense to proactively spend a portion of your healthcare spend on measures that could positively affect that spend over time?

Our challenge is the desire for instant gratification. This drive emerges primarily from two groups: financial managers and end users.

Financial Managers: Challenges to See the ROI

The financial managers – such as the CFO and CEO – may initially see wellness as just another overhead expenditure. Depending on how you present the concept of wellness, it may come across as another "soft" program that is "touchy, feely" and has no impact on the bottom line of the business. Hopefully, your business leadership is more in-tune to the correlation between employee health and business performance, but you cannot make that assumption. Many still don't understand it.

You will need to demonstrate the ROI of this program.

Many wellness research sources indicate that it will take 3-5 years to demonstrate a return on investment from wellness. When financial managers hear this, they become uneasy. They want to see instant ROI. I am not clear about what makes wellness different from any other investment that they make. It takes time to see a *return* on the investment. First, it takes money to make money, so we need investment in the program. Second, the size of the return is *directly* proportionate to the size of the investment. Third, there is no such thing as instant gratification in smart investment strategy. Sure, now and then someone may hit the jackpot with the surprise IPO or stock split, but for the rest of the world, that doesn't happen. It takes time. The same goes for wellness.

It will take some time, but if you implement the program the right way – find your support base, launch the education, and create a true partnership – the ROI will become visible quickly. I have yet to do this and not see the ROI within the **first year**. That's not a guarantee of course, but that is just from my experience. The ROI comes in the forms of lower experience from reduced claims, fewer accidents, changed behavior, improved consumerism, and other changes. In the first year alone, the number of emergency room visits dropped by 50%, much of

114

which can be attributed to an increase in urgent care facilities instead. That saved us thousands and thousands of dollars.

When discussing the program with the CFO or other executives, be sure to speak in their language. Use specific, measurable criteria that will make the difference between earning their support or passing this program off as just another overhead expense.

Identify your claims year over year. Do not just speak in terms of percentages. Those are easy. Instead, convert that information to dollars – how much each increase costs, what that increase has cost year over year, and the total increase in healthcare spending over the past ten years. Then identify what the continued accumulated cost of each new increase is as you move forward...1% today will be 1% tomorrow and forever into the future. The more specific your numbers, the better you can identify your challenges.

When demonstrating the probable savings in the future, consider the impact on claims. What does a 1% reduction in claims look like? Quantify it and show how it can happen. Also consider other implications of your program, including:

- Improved morale
- Increased productivity
- Decrease in absenteeism
- Enhanced retention

As you are better able to add numbers to each of these potential outcomes of your plan, these can be additional selling points to your program. The key is to avoid overselling while at the same time adding up everything that you should be receiving credit for when proposing such an integrated program.

Employees: Challenges to See the Results
Employees are also looking for proof – proof that this program can do what it says that it will. Social proof will help as employees seek validation for (or against) your plan as a solution for their challenges.

Financially, employees want to know how you will make or save THEM money - directly. Talking about the company saving money isn't motivational. Even talking about saving the health plan money and how those savings help to pass the cost savings to everyone in the future is not a compelling reason to make changes in behavior. People need to know what's in it for them.

The program needs to speak to them directly in two ways – how it will earn them (a) more money and (b) better health.

The "more money" element comes from either making money or saving money. If the plan will make employees money (e.g., employer paid HSA contributions, interest, and growth from HSA investments) or save them money (e.g., fewer claims costs, less severity of claims, lower overall costs with fewer claims), and you can show them how, this will generally earn their attention.

The "better health" sell is a bit tougher. Everyone has heard for years that they should get into shape, eat less, exercise more, or other messaging about becoming healthy. Having the employer chime in is just one more voice. However, if there is an internal momentum to increase overall health and wellbeing, you will start to see the shift take place. Remember – people spend more waking hours at work than they do anywhere else. If you can set the tone and message in the workplace, you can adjust the tone and perspective for them when they aren't at work.

Meaningful Rewards Based Program

The incentives must be large enough to motivate and generate shifts in behavior. Offering t-shirts and water bottles are fun, but they are not motivational enough to fundamentally change the behavior over time that will make the difference you need. Consider the following.

- **Reward vs. Penalty Based Program**

    Two things motivate us: pain and pleasure. Pain is more effective in the short-term, but pleasure is far more effective as a motivator over time. Think about it. How many times do you hear "do this or else" before you tire of it and you say, "OK - I'll take the 'or else' to make you quiet!"

    That happens with healthcare as well. The ones who are going to do it will do it and those who won't do it, won't. Offering a reward for helping is much more palatable than making people feel that they dodged a bullet. At the same time, you want those who are not helping to feel the "pain" and to know that they are feeling it because they didn't help. We can summarize both in how we define "rewards" with employees. For example:

    o   Annual wellness incentives of up to $2,700 go to employee Health Savings Accounts for meeting biometric requirements for things such as blood pressure, blood sugar, body mass/weight, and cholesterol or completing a reasonable alternative.

    o   Employees receive a $600/year "tobacco discount" off their premiums for passing a cotinine test (or completing the reasonable alternative).

    In the first example, it truly is a reward because the employee starts with nothing and gets "something" by completing the requirements. The second example is one where we take a "penalty" for using tobacco and apply it as a discount. Rather than starting with a lower insurance rate and applying a penalty,

117

we raised the "base" rate and applied a discount instead. Much more palatable.

- **Significant Rewards**

Here's the secret when it comes to making wellness work:

You can't get million-dollar results
with $5 gift cards.

Seriously. I speak with CFOs all the time as they try to understand the "secret" to our success, and I let them know the magic...I give the money back to the employees. They are confused. We lower premiums, give the money we save by raising deductibles back to the employees and still save money. How does that work?

Enter the world of "Wade-o-nomics."

Of course, it doesn't make sense. However, neither does common core math.

When you give employees the money back, and you educate them to become better consumers, they become stingy and start making better decisions. They begin to take better care of themselves and focus more on better living. Providing the funds to the employees to manage helps them to become users and managers of their assets, and, rather than me trying to control the program myself, I now have hundreds of users who are individually managing the program.

How?

They are making better choices so they can keep their money as long as possible. As they find new ways to earn money, save money, and reduce their costs over time, they will continue to be a strategic partner to reduce costs.

Genius.

- **Choice**

Your wellness program must have choice built into the program. People always need an alternative. Even if the second choice is a terrible choice, there is a fundamental human need to have a choice. Otherwise, we tend to resist change if it appears to be inherently less attractive.

In the case of a wellness program, it is up to us to create the option that makes so much sense; it would be ridiculous to choose otherwise. Forcing everyone into a single choice – say, into a high deductible plan – will force resistance. Even if it is the best option available for everyone, the fact that you took away choice creates the basic need to resist.

Several will argue with me that by maintaining a PPO plan when rolling out a high deductible plan, people will naturally gravitate towards the PPO plan because it is what they know. It is natural, comfortable, and more relaxed. I do not disagree. That being the case, let's create a situation where employees MUST take a second look at the HDHP before they settle in on the final decision. For example:

   o **Premiums**: Setting a premium for your high deductible plan that is so much lower than the PPO plan that it draws their attention is a great way to start. In Year 1, we dropped the premiums by 15%. What happens next is where the genius sets in. As we saved money through the program, we continued to attack the employee contribution rates, but we limited it ONLY to the HDHP program. As we saved money, we left the PPO rates alone. Zero increase for PPO members was still a "win," but in Year 2, we dropped the HDHP rates by another 10%. With a 25% differential, they had to start to do the math. Entering Year 3, we had saved over $2M, so we dropped family rates by $100/mo. and employee + spouse and + kids by $50/mo. This left rates at LESS THAN HALF of the PPO rates. We still have 40% on the PPO plan, but we do have 60% taking advantage of the lower rates. Change takes time. In the meantime, those paying extra for premiums are helping to fund all the other programs we have going on.

- o **HSA Contributions**: I've shared it before, but a big part of the program is the incentive program. Employees can earn the ENTIRE deductible back in wellness incentives under our plan. Also, THE SPOUSE can earn the deductible, resulting in $0 personal cost for the deductible out of their own pockets for a high deductible health plan each year if they participate. Cool, right?

  Then when you add that to the lower premiums, there is not a scenario out there where the PPO is more advantageous to the HDHP program. We preach it, we do the math, we walk employees through it, and still, we have 40% in the PPO program.

  And that's OK. We try. We're getting there.

- **Tracking and Automation**
  As you can imagine, with this many moving parts, it can become easy to be overwhelmed to think of the administration to track points, rewards, etc. if you did this all manually. It makes my head spin just thinking of some poor soul trying to track everything by spreadsheet. That is before I think of the exposure to personal health information and how to manage that mess with all the documentation floating around.

  To make the program work, you need a system to track and automate what you are doing. There are several options out there to help. Many are on the market that integrate nicely with other systems, track points, and communicate with other vendors.

  For example, in our system, as employees complete wellness requirements (e.g., biometrics), they earn points in the wellness platform. At the end of each month, the points tally is sent over to our HSA vendor who then pulls money from our bank and funds the HSA accounts accordingly. This automated system allows us to facilitate an otherwise complicated process with minimal staff attention to the details.

Wellness Committee

A key to any functioning wellness program is the use of a wellness committee. Most people (me included) want to have control over the program, at least to start. We like control, so we can ensure that the involvement is "just right." Giving up control from the start is uncomfortable. What we need to understand is that the sooner we can help others take over, the better the program will be.

The Wellness Committee is an excellent opportunity to engage your workplace as it is generally made up of representatives from around the company. Much like the Safety Committee should represent the company's interests, so too can the Wellness Committee bring in a broad perspective of ideas, interests, and opinions on how to implement and integrate wellness throughout the company. The Committee is also a great group of volunteers upon whom you can depend for activities, events, and assistance throughout the year.

I have generally chaired the Wellness Committee for the first year to provide an example and a model for the committee members to watch. After the first year, I hand the role of the chair over to another employee. I generally step off the committee and let another member of HR represent the interests of the department, which allows the employees to feel a bit more autonomous with the activity arm of the program. I still run the incentives and structural elements of the program. However, the activities such as the Summer Olympics, lunch and learns, weight loss challenges, step competitions, softball teams, etc. are all in the hands of the employees. I fund the activities and awards. It's one less thing for me to worry about because it "just happens" and the employees do a great job of managing it. They are engaged, employees love it, we have a great time.

Outcomes Based

With such a significant investment in wellness, it makes sense to want a return on that investment. The more we give, the more we should be willing to ask in return, right? Part of that "ask" is for "outcomes" which may be a delicate topic if you don't approach this the right way, which is why I recommend offering a gob of money. The more you give, the more you can ask.

That said, there is also the risk of what you can and cannot offer when constrained by all the regulation. In the case of the EEOC, it may be the "absence" of regulation. At the time of this book's publication, we are still waiting to hear an opinion that has been lingering for a year and a half to determine whether outcomes-based incentives will continue to be allowed. Some employers have decided to play it safe and give up any outcomes-based incentives to avoid the potential for any problems in the future. That's nice. I'm continuing to do it until I see the results because this is where we make the most significant difference. Even if they come back and say that we shouldn't, I'm waiting until the definitive 'NO' before I stop.

For those wondering what I'm talking about, an "outcomes-based" approach is rewarding employees based on the outcomes of their biometrics. If an employee meets the standards for their four basic biometrics, they receive the reward. So, if an employee meets the established criteria for his or her weight given their height, gender, and age, they receive a contribution to their health savings account (HSA). If they do not meet the standards, they can still complete a "reasonable alternative" by EITHER losing 5% of his or her body weight OR lose 3% and complete a 6-session telephonic coaching program by December 31st of the current calendar year. We have three other biometric standards for blood pressure, blood sugar, and cholesterol.

It's doable. The employee must complete these standards to earn the reward. If married, the spouse can complete it as well to receive the reward. In the end, we ask for a lot; however, we give a lot. We allow the employee to earn the ENTIRE deductible back - up to $1,350. The spouse can also earn up to $1,350 to cover the deductible for him/her for a total of $2,700. With that much money on the line, shouldn't we be able to ask for the employee to have some actual results from their efforts?

This example demonstrates how we reward those who contribute to the solution. Again, those who do not pass the tests can complete reasonable alternatives. Several do it…they are not impossible, and there are several options for those who are disabled. Many choose not to do it.

Activities

An active approach must drive the wellness program to promote behavior that addresses critical health priorities among your employees. Given the diverse nature of employee groups, these needs will be as unique as you are.

Wellness cannot happen from behind the desk.

You can have games, videos, instructions, and other things that come via email, portals, and online platforms. That's nice…but real engagement, and culture change comes from your ability to drive change at the core. Movement and behavior shift must come from a fundamental level that requires ongoing commitment and development. I am not necessarily promoting group exercises for everyone at the start of the shift (although studies have shown that can be beneficial BTW!!). What I am saying is that you need a program that is active and offers several options to connect something to everyone.

Promoting "Wellness Your Way"
I am confident that I didn't coin the phrase years ago when I called the first wellness program that I put together "Wellness Your Way," but it sticks well. The concept is simple. Provide enough opportunities for employees to build their wellness program that fits their lifestyle, interests, time, condition, etc. It goes back to the age-old question: What's the best exercise? Answer: The one that you'll do. Let's provide options for our employees to help them move and become engaged in the behavior changes that make sense.

Creating Options
There are plenty of books and resources out there that provide ideas and lists of specific activities you can launch. That is not the purpose of this book. Creating a comprehensive list of options has been done multiple times, and you can do a little homework to receive a plethora of ideas. However, let me share a few of the things that have worked well for my employees, and some of the lessons learned as we have implemented them.

- **Onsite Biometrics**: We build biometrics into our wellness incentives, so we provide onsite biometrics onsite to remove any excuses or barriers to participating. Sure, they can go to their doctor and complete it if they want. No problem. However, we also offer it onsite to provide convenience. Given that the spouse is also eligible to earn points and incentives for biometric results, we also provide spouses the opportunity to come onsite to complete their biometrics at no cost as well. (BTW…we cover the cost of onsite biometrics through the extra funds paid by those who do not qualify for our tobacco discount. BTW#2…we bring in biometrics vendors who talk directly to our online wellness platform to upload points and results and thereby avoid our managing personal health information.)

- **Weight Loss / Maintenance Challenge**: Most places have some "Biggest Loser" competition. What we found is that the people who are in shape or have nothing to lose also want to play, so we also include an option for those who meet the BMI standards. Not only do we reward the "losers" for losing the weight with points through the platform, but we also reward individuals who already meet BMI standards that maintain their weight through the competition. They can participate, have fun, earn points, and gain rewards for being part of the solution.

- **"Maintain…Don't Gain"**: One of the most popular activities happens during the winter holidays. The weight "loss" competition occurs in the early spring in time to get ready for spring. The winter season has a "maintain, don't gain" program, so employees avoid overeating and watch their health through the holidays. It has proven to be very successful in promoting healthy lifestyles through the holidays.

- **Wellness Fair**: Offering an annual wellness fair where we bring the carriers, vendors, and even providers on site to meet with employees and their spouses is a hit. It provides a fun environment that promotes healthy living and a great chance to ask questions, obtain resources, and learn about resources available to them.

- **Lunch and Learns**: About ten times a year, we offer a series of lunch and learns, typically provided by local vendors who come in to provide insights, information, and tips on all-things wellness. Topics may include healthy eating, building an exercise program, preparing for spring sports, and healthy weight loss. We also bring in other support from other areas of wellness such as counselors from the Employee Assistance Program (EAPP to talk about managing stress and anxiety (mental and emotional wellness) as well as representatives from local credit unions to share tips about buying a house, repairing credit, or building a reliable savings program (financial wellness).

- **Steps Competition**: Through our online platform, we can coordinate steps challenges among employees who have connected their wearable devices. The platform allows multiple brands of devices to sync steps (to calculate points for stepping), which then allows us to bring hundreds of employees together for stepping competitions as individuals or teams.

- **Healthy Eating Options**: You can build healthy eating options into your existing programs. For example, our monthly employee barbecue didn't change, but we were able to build in healthy options of veggie burgers and offering carrots, celery and grapes as sides (vs. just chips in the past). We also expanded new categories into the annual chili cook-off to include a healthy category.

- **Office Olympics**: These may originate during an Olympic year, or not, but they will remain forever if you let them. Each summer we allowed a period for a week where teams competed for a half hour each day, culminating in an awards ceremony at the end of the week. It is a great time and a new tradition.

- **Outside Team Events**: We sponsor the softball team in the local league of employees and spouses. We also sponsor several teams in the local annual mini-marathon. As events arise, we encourage participation to promote individuals and families to participate in outside activities.

The list does go on and on. These are just a few of our events. Bringing in an active wellness committee to support, organize, and facilitate these events is critical to encourage participation and avoid having to spend your entire time facilitating activities. You really can make this work even with a skeleton crew, light budget, and little administrative support when you show the vision and light a fire of motivation and encouragement in a well-structured and planned program.

One Example: Integrated Wellness at Wagstaff, Inc.

The value of case studies is to provide an opportunity to learn from others. It is not necessary to demonstrate perfection because there are always opportunities to improve. No two companies are the same, and no situations are going to match precisely. That said, let's share the experience of Wagstaff.

Wagstaff is a mid-size, 70+-year-old family-owned manufacturing company in the aluminum industry with 500 employees. Before beginning, they had a fully funded PPO program and had faced double-digit increases at renewals for several years. Like most employers, they had mitigated cost increases with costs sharing with employees, increase premiums, and benefits reductions (e.g., increased deductibles, increased co-pays, reduced coverage, etc.).

In year one, the renewals were facing another double-digit increase. The company prepared to embrace more of the same. Through a partnership with Mercer and ongoing negotiations with the carrier, I was able to present a proposal of a coordinated wellness program to implement at the company based upon a successful program implemented just a few years prior with another local employer. With promises of fully engaged employees, investment from the employer (which I admittedly had not secured yet), and projected cost savings through the drafted strategy, we were able to negotiate a much lower renewal than expected.

Shocked that it worked and knowing that it was on negotiation and goodwill alone, I took the results back to management and made a request. The company could have taken the money it saved and ran with it. Instead, they asked me how much I needed and the purpose of the funds. We had budgeted 20% for the increase we expected. The net increase was 4%. I asked for 4% back. They were, of course, in a good mood, so that was the time to ask. I asked for 2% to build an on-site gym and 2% for ongoing wellness expenses. There's nothing like installing an on-site gym to say that you're serious about your commitment to wellness. With the other 2%, I had the working capital to implement the online wellness platform and launched the operating expenses for promotions, swag, and other things related to wellness.

YEAR 1: WELLNESS ROLL-OUT
We were still fully funded in that first year, but we launched the full wellness program without integrated incentives into the insurance plan. As we rolled out the open enrollment for the year, we did educate on the value of wellness, the incentives inherent within the online platform, and the opportunity to make a difference in the claims over the next year. We began the active education process of employees and throughout the challenge to make a difference, and with that difference, we could take a bite out of the renewals for the following year. The Wellness Committee went to work, everything launched, and people became very active. Over the course of the first year, the behavior changed well enough that the claims dropped significantly and put us in place to become self-insured the following year.

YEAR 2: SELF-FUNDING/WELLNESS INTEGRATION
Once we were self-insured, it made sense for us to roll out the high deductible program. We maintained the PPO program as well, but both programs rolled into the same coverage. Both were still covered under the same carrier in the same plan, just with different entry points at the front end. We have consistently dropped the rates of the high deductible plan for employees with the intent to draw more participants to that plan. We are now at the point where the high deductible family premium is less than half of the PPO family plan for the same coverage except for the deductible. Also, employees can earn back the entire deductible through wellness incentives, as explained below. Still, I only have 60% of employees who have selected the HSA option.

Many on the outside (and on the inside) have asked why I don't merely drop the PPO plan altogether. I have found that no matter what, people want a choice. Even if the other option is a bad choice, people still want a choice. We find that so long as they have a choice, they have something to choose. The perception of simple is enough to make them happy, and they will pay for it. No matter how much we have done to simplify the process of educating them on what they can do to save money, we have at least given them a choice, and they are taking it.

STEP 1: TOBACCO
The first step of the program was to address the behavior that is easiest to modify that affects our trends, perhaps the most – tobacco use. Regardless of the plan – PPO or high deductible – tobacco users contribute unnecessarily to increased costs associated with cancers, lung

129

disease, and the plethora of other healthcare related expenses. Rather than apply a "penalty" to users, we decided to provide a "reward" to nonusers. We did this by rolling out a new set of insurance rates that were substantially higher and then offering a "discount" to nontobacco users. To verify that they do not use tobacco, employees need to pass a cotinine screen test. These are provided on-site before open enrollment at various times through the winter and spring at no cost to the employees. If the employee has a spouse on the plan, they are also required to take the test and pass it or complete a reasonable alternative by the designated deadline. The premium discount is in the amount of **$600 per year**. If you want the behavior to change, you need to make the incentive large enough to make it worth their while. We thought that $600 was worth their while.

STEP 2: WELLNESS (PPO)

The second step of the program was to address wellness. For those on the PPO plan, we still wanted to incentivize those individuals with a wellness option. Individuals who complete their biometrics receive a $300 discount off their premiums per year. We do not go off results in the case of PPO participants – they must complete their biometric screening to receive the incentive. We even offered the biometric screening on-site at no cost to the employees several times during the winter and spring months before the completion of open enrollment. All they need to do is show up and have it done, and they can receive a $300 discount. It sounded fair to us, but many still pass on this discount.

STEP 3: WELLNESS (HIGH DEDUCTIBLE)

Because wellness is at the core of the behavior change, we can offer significant incentives to those on the high deductible plan. The first incentive is a cost differential to the premium. If that premium differential is wide enough, it should start to earn the attention of the employee, and at this point, the employee only rate is practically free, and the family rate is less than half of the cost than the PPO rate.

The other incentive to attract participants into the high deductible plan is through wellness incentives. An individual on the high deductible plan can earn back their entire deductible through wellness incentives. In addition, if the employee has a spouse on the program, the spouse can also earn their deductible as well.

We wanted to make participation as easy as possible and reduce the barriers to entry. Having a high deductible plan was a new thing for the organization. As such, we made the deductible as low as possible. We also had the fewest number of deductibles per family (2). With the lowest point of entry, and the easiest approach to begin, we also wanted to offer employees the opportunity to earn the ENTIRE deductible back through wellness incentives.

Currently, employees can earn the deductible back for themselves, and if they are married, their spouse can also earn the entire incentives back for him or her as well. At the time of publication, the minimum deductible is $1,350 for a combined total of $2,700 available to be earned by the employee and his or her spouse per year through wellness contributions into the health savings account. Not only do they save thousands on premiums, but they also earn thousands in their HSA's through wellness contributions. We are giving away free money.

STEP 4: INCENTIVES
As part of the strategy, it is essential to provide substantial enough incentives to motivate behavior change. The following outlines the incentives for employees to earn $1,350 as part of the HSA incentives.

$200   Complete the biometrics assessment

$100   Meet standards for blood sugar (A1C or standard blood sugar)

$100   Meet standards for blood pressure

$100   Meet standards for cholesterol

$100   Meet standards for BMI

$200   Complete and pass all standards for biometrics

$200 Achieve Gold level within the Online Platform

$350 Achieve Platinum level within the Online Platform

All biometric standards run through the online platform. Those who do not pass a given measure can achieve a reasonable alternative managed through the online platform. Gold and Platinum levels within the online platform also contribute to the points accumulation.

As employees earn points through the online platform, points accumulate for use towards wellness status. At the end of each month, reports generate to ABG. Those individuals who have achieved certain levels and qualified for HSA contributions will receive those contributions monthly. All measures and payments automate with monthly reconciliation through HR.

SUMMARY
There are, of course, active functions that take place throughout the year with the support of the wellness committee. We have active campaigns, weight loss challenges, step challenges, and other features and functions that are taking place to keep wellness and health at the forefront of everyone's mind throughout the year. As we maintain transparency and open communication and then sponsor ongoing activities to keep people healthy, momentum is sustained, and changes in behavior continue.

NEW MINDSETS

Doing Things Differently

Up to this point in the book – if you're still with me – you may be thinking, "This is great, Wade, but this is old school. We know this stuff already. Nothing new here." If that is the case, I would ask if you're doing it. If so and you're rocking it on your results, fantastic. Congrats.

If you're like most folks, you'll give me the same complaint or tell me that this is the "same 'ol stuff," that you've heard before - but then share that you haven't implemented it. That's a more common response. At that point, I share that you cannot expect to earn the same as we did by just passing out t-shirts and skimping on the rest. It doesn't work that way. It takes a full commitment…not just dabbling and then saying, *"Wellness doesn't work. We tried it once, and it didn't work for us."*

Yeah, I hear that a lot.

Now, if you're past the basics and you're looking for the next level solutions that can create the next level of results, you've come to the right section. Please note that you cannot just jump to the back of the book and implement these ideas by themselves and expect to find healthcare nirvana. These are only a few more tools to add to your arsenal.

No single idea presented here or anywhere else is going to be the magic ticket to fix healthcare for your company.

It is going to take a well-concerted, multi-faceted approach to fix a complex problem that has taken us years to create.

With that preparation, let's talk about what it does take to make the change happen. It's going to take a new mindset. Period. We cannot keep doing things the same old way and expect different results. (Insanity anyone?) The current situation is desperate and calls for change – massive change. Not ridiculous change – not stupid change. Just massive change from what we've done before and that will require a new way of seeing the world, of thinking about healthcare and of managing the business of healthcare.

Welcome to the Game

I shared at the introduction of the book that healthcare is a game - it is. Like it or not, you're being played, and you can continue to be played, or you can begin to be a real player in the game. As I mentioned, the ones who learn the rules of the game will win. Those who do not learn how to play the game – the full game – will not be successful.

As a game, you must understand that it is more like a casino with multiple games being played simultaneously. You have a choice as to which games you would like to play. Some of us may only know the game that is in front of us, and we may only want to stay with that game. So be it. When you go to Vegas, you may only want to play the slots. Some slots are luckier than others. However, there are many other games around, and you may have a chance to win at those if you know the rules of those games, know how to play, and can successfully navigate them.

So, within this same analogy, does that mean that every new thing we try will work out? No. Sometimes we'll lose, or it won't work. The new approach may fail. There is risk involved in some of these. However, one thing is for sure – we know what we have right now, and it's not working. Something must change, and no one will do it for us. We need to find a different way.

A New Mindset

A new mindset requires a new way of seeing, thinking, and acting. The handful of ideas presented in the next sections are options that I have put in place that served my organization well to varying degrees. They may not be the right solution for you. Taking on a new mindset means asking the question "What if?" rather than merely shutting down new ideas. Moving your mindset from "If" to "How" creates a solution orientation so it's never whether you can do something - but how you're going to do something.

"Growth is painful. Change is painful. However, nothing is as painful as staying stuck somewhere you don't belong..."

Pharmacy Carve-Out

If you are going to manage your costs, you must explicitly and independently manage each of your significant costs. That means you must be able to carve out your pharmacy by itself. You may receive a great deal from the medical side to bundle pharma. If so, great. They will promise the "best" negotiated prices, best contracts, and best rebates (if you're self-funded). In the end, if they are managing your pharma with your medical, there is a good chance that you are not receiving the best deal.

If you are fully funded, you can't do this. Period.

If you are self-funded, it will depend entirely on who is managing the third-party administration. If you are having your carrier also serve as your third-party administrator, good luck. They may not allow you to carve out anything. I found myself hostage for the first couple of years after the last move to self-funding. I knew I would be going in and did it anyway due to the management of the change process (I had to manage just how much disruption I brought on at one time).

As you evaluate programs at the end of each year, it will be worth your while to run the analysis to see what it might do if you pulled out pharma to run independently. The last time we did, we found that we could have access to the same pharmacy network with the same plan design...and still *save hundreds of thousands of dollars.*

Programs with the best results have found it to be far more effective to carve out their pharmacy coverage from their medical plan and go out to bid separately for pharmacy benefits. This approach allows for a few things:

- Pharmacy benefits providers can focus on one thing – providing the best pharmacy benefits possible.

- Separate programs may provide greater flexibility in your plan design specific to pharmacy benefits, especially for specialty drugs.

137

- Many third-party administrators (TPAs) can bundle billing and administration for both medical and pharmacy into a single bill.

Give it a try. See for yourself. Carving it out may be a solution that can save you and your plan a tremendous amount of money.

Medical Tourism

Medical tourism is merely sending an individual off to another location to receive medical care. It is often associated with international medical tourism, which involves travel to another country for a surgical procedure or treatment. Why would someone consider this? Cost. In most cases, they can have a procedure done in another country for a fraction of the cost of having the same procedure – with the same technology, same parts, same outcomes.

The idea of medical tourism is not new, I admit. However, how many are doing it? Not many. We still stick around and pay full price for medical procedures and then complain about the cost. With advances in technology and global travel, it has become easier than ever before to receive medical services around the globe. Doctors in other countries come to the United States for medical training and are internationally accredited to perform these same procedures with stellar results. Still, there is often a mindset that we can only have these procedures done in the United States.

Even within the U.S., we consider surgical procedures and treatment options as commodities…that the services we receive from one doctor are the same or equivalent to the services that we receive from anyone else. Of course, we like our doctor – we trust our doctor. However, are we receiving the BEST service? Will we be receiving the very best surgical option by using our physician? How do you know?

Most patients have not spent any time at all asking these questions. They go with what their doctor tells them and follow the instructions the first time through. If they are not working directly with a surgeon, they go to the surgeon recommended by their primary care doctor and do not ask for second opinions or ask whether the surgeon they are seeing is the best option for their situation. Is the surgeon the best option? How much will the surgery cost? How do the cost and quality compare to other surgeons in the area? Could you find a better surgeon in the area? Is there another option that can improve both price and quality? These are foreign concepts.

When you think about it, you spend far more time asking these kinds of questions about a used car then you ever would about your body. However, your vehicle will last a few years at best, and then it'll be gone. Your body must last the rest of your life. We'll spend far more time researching the cost and value of a television than we will a doctor.

Medical tourism puts consumerism back in your hands to give you options to consider BOTH cost and quality. Combined, this creates value to the consumer and the company. You can create a value proposition that motivates employees to consider ways to improve the outcomes by working with you to find alternatives to the "same 'ol thing" by creating solutions to better care at a better cost. In return, you can develop solutions for the employee and his or her family that make sense and create a benefit that works for everyone.

- **Domestic Medical Tourism**

  Medical tourism doesn't have to take you out of the country. For example, it may make sense to send a patient to the Mayo Clinic or Cleveland Clinic for a condition because they are the best in the country. Yes, it will cost more to fly them there and put them up in a hotel for them and their spouse. However, if they can perform a better surgery, have better outcomes that result in faster healing, fix the problem completely, have a lower probability of post-surgical infection, and keep it at the same cost as a local hospital, why wouldn't you do it?

  As we were researching options to identify new solutions, we came across a local private hospital that was outside the traditional networks. Northwest Specialty Hospital in Post Falls, Idaho was set up by design to accommodate medical tourism from Canadians seeking medical care they could not obtain in their own country. As a private hospital, they were not subject to the same requirements as the other hospitals with emergency rooms, so their cost structure was different, saving tremendous overhead to their model.

  I was able to negotiate a significant discount directly with this hospital that was only 20-miles away. They serve us for radiology (MRIs especially), surgeries, and several services. Because of the discount, I can offer the service to employees at no cost – I wave the copays and coinsurance (of course, HSA employees need to meet the deductible first). This explanation is perhaps the shortest version of domestic medical tourism on the books.

Still, it may be more cost effective to find a Center of Excellence for a specific medical procedure and pay for the individual to travel to that location. While it may seem to cost more initially, you have the potential to save money from fewer complications, faster healing, and better quality overall.

If you have the capacity and can build it in, it may make sense to offer domestic medical tourism to your employees for surgeries to be conducted by top doctors in top locations for the same or lower costs — just a thought.

- **International Medical Tourism**

The more commonly thought of approach to medical tourism involves international sources of medical services. In short, individuals seek medical services from providers in other countries for a fraction of the price they would pay for it in the U.S.

The most common concern that people have with medical tourism is quality of care: is it safe? That's a valid concern. It is critical to understand that price is not everything. Sure, it sounds like a great deal to receive a knee replacement for $20,000. However, it is essential to understand how to go about finding the right ways to ensure safe, reliable, and high-quality options.

International accreditation through JCI is a great way to verify quality standards. Much like our rules are followed in the U.S., international accreditation bodies such as JCI ensure high standards of care. Other measures may be obtained that you can consider as well by an institution that you may take into consideration.

We had a great experience with CIMA Hospital in San Jose, Costa Rica. I was invited to visit San Jose and review the facilities of a few hospitals and facilities. While all of them were

141

admirable in their approaches, CIMA came out ahead in their service and quality standards. As I shared in the story about my journey, I even used them for my procedure. High quality, excellent care, fantastic service - AND save us a bunch of money? That's just good business.

Direct Billing Relationships

The latest trend is to build a direct billing relationship with providers – hospitals, physicians, and other providers of healthcare. Employers have found opportunities to build relationships directly with providers by incentivizing utilization at a facility, receiving a discounted rate, and in exchange, directly paying for all services.

For the employer, the pricing makes all the difference. By working directly with the carrier, the employer can save a tremendous amount on the cost of the services and the amount billed for each service. It may be as inexpensive as 50% off the cash price offered publicly or more. When compared to the billed rates for procedures, this can add up to a lot of money throughout the year for the employer with enough volume.

For the provider, this relationship makes sense for several reasons. First, they are paid sooner...a lot sooner. Once a bill is processed for a patient, it may take 90-days or longer before a carrier pays - if it is not initially denied and thereby require additional paperwork, time and effort to file the denials. Second, they are paid more, and more consistently. By offering a single cash price, the employer pays less, and the carrier receives less cash but is required to spend significantly less processing time to pay the money out. By cutting the "red tape," they save personnel costs that would have otherwise been spent processing bills.

Employers may offer several incentives to employees to use these locations with the negotiated prices. For example, I've offered **no copays/coinsurance**. For PPO members or HDHP members who have met their deductible, the company picks up all additional costs, which makes the MRI, surgery, etc. "free" to the employee. This option can save employees hundreds or even thousands of dollars per year.

These direct contracting relationships are becoming common, and employers are starting to ask the question, "Why do we need [CONSULTANTS]?" Employers need to be smarter. Brokers need to be providing solutions year-round and not just once a year when it's convenient. Direct billing contracts may become more and more prevalent as both sides of the equation (employer and provider) benefit greatly by them.

Pharmacy Tourism

Last year, I was meeting with my medical concierge from Medical Travel Option over lunch about new opportunities available to me. During our lunch conversation, she shared with me her experience with another facility in Mexico and their experience with specialty medications. They have been working with employers to bring employees across the border into Tijuana for access to specialty medications from the same manufacturers for significantly lower prices.

Here's the story behind it. At the printing of this book, it is legal to transport a 90-day supply of medication over the border from Mexico to the United States per day for yourself. The drug must be for a condition for which the individual receives treatment, a physician in Mexico must issue the medication, and the individual must have a copy of the prescription for the drug.

While other companies do it, we worked with Provide Rx through Hospital Angeles in Tijuana. They assist with ordering the medication directly from the manufacturer – the same manufacturer that makes the drug for us here in the United States. We are merely avoiding the American markup on the drug.

On our side of the border, an employee can volunteer to participate in the program. (We will talk about the incentives to participate in a moment.) The employee must present to us a copy of a valid US passport – crossing the border into Mexico isn't a problem. We need to make sure they can return to the U.S. They also need to provide to us a copy of a 90-day prescription (or multiple 90-day prescriptions depending upon the length of time that they are going to travel) from their doctor here in the United States to validate their condition and to initiate the order of the medication. We send these documents over to Provide Rx to begin the process.

At this point, Provide Rx issues an invoice. We wire the funds directly to the corporate account for Provide Rx located in the United States in US dollars, they order the medication and make all the necessary arrangements on the Mexican side of the border. They also make the arrangements with the Mexican physician who will provide a basic examination of the patient when they arrived to verify the need for treatment. This process is not to second-guess the will of the American physician, but rather to provide validation per Mexican law before issuing the medication on that side of the border.

With money transferred and medication ordered, we prepare for the employee to travel. Our medical concierge handles all the arrangements for travel. As a company, we pay for the flight as well as the concierge services. To make the trip even more worthwhile, it makes sense for us to send the employee down for two days. That way, they can go down on one day, received the first 90-day supply, come back and stay overnight in San Diego, go back the next day for a second 90-day supply, and then fly back home. In that case, we also pay for the hotel accommodations in downtown San Diego.

Once the employee lands at the San Diego airport, a transport company ask them up from the airport and transports them directly to the hospital where representatives from Provide RX meet them. The transportation company will shuttle them back and forth between San Diego and Tijuana on both days. This way, we as the employer do not need to worry about anything. The employee does not need to worry about anything. Our needs are met.

So why do something like this?

From the employee's perspective, it is noble of them to help us out, but there are some cost savings to them. As the employer, we waive all the co-pays for the employees on the PPO plan. For these drugs are on a more expensive tier of co-pays, this can save the employee hundreds of dollars a year. For individuals on the high deductible plan, they will need to have met their deductible before we can cover this for them. However, once they have reached their deductible, we will offer the same by covering all co-pays and coinsurance is for their medications.

In addition to this, many find it fun to travel. Employees can use their sick leave – which is often never used for healthy employees. This allows them to travel, especially in the wintertime to somewhere warmer. We cover all the travel costs, and they can go somewhere fun.

Finally, employees can make up to $2000 a year cash for taking advantage of this program. We pay employees $500 per 90-days prescription that they complete. So, for those who go down for a two-day trip to fill for a 180-day supply of medications, that will earn them $1000 extra money. This way, they save hundreds on co-pays and earn a couple of thousand dollars directly from cash contributions. Not bad.

Moreover, why would an employer offer something like this? These medications cost the plan thousands of dollars a month for an individual. The cost difference to have this filled in Mexico is as much as 60 to 70% less. After all the costs are taken into consideration, this still saves the company tens of thousands of dollars per year per person compared to what it was pain before through the standard pharmacy plan.

Does this sound a little bit too far out of the box for you? Consider this – the State of Utah recently adopted this as its primary strategy for all its employees. Employees can still choose to receive their medications domestically, but it will cost them substantially more than if they take advantage of this program offered by the State. We adopted a similar strategy with our cost structure. They can still fill it domestically, but it is going to cost them significantly more to do so.

When it comes to creating your incentive strategy to control costs and change behavior, remember:

You can lead a horse to water, but you can't make it drink. But you can put salt in its oats...

The key is to keep putting salt in the oats. Eventually, they will become thirsty, and they will become more interested in the water that you are serving.

Stop Loss Captives

You may be familiar with captives that are used within the L&I world for workers' compensation. It's the same concept — a group of like-minded employers pools their resources to self-fund risk as a group. As the performance of the captive does well, the members of the captive may split earnings distributions. Similarly, when the performance of the captive does not do so well, the group bears the risk together.

Traditional stop-loss coverage works just like fully funded insurance. You pay the premium, it dictates the terms of your insurance coverage, and that's that. Pray that nothing hits. Even if you don't have a claim hit your stop loss, you may still receive an increase to your premiums due to what *they* believe is an increase in risk.

In a captive, the general approach is to pool the money with other smaller employers (maybe employers of a few hundred to a few thousand) to share the risk of reinsurance. Employers may be expected to post some form of collateral to cover an anomaly that may arise, such as a case of cancer or unexpected accident. They may be expected to contribute an extra $50,000 up front in case situations don't go according to plans or projections as part of an initial "buy-in" to join with an investment.

From there, in most situations, the captive member typically joins in the management of the investment to help the money work in the advantage of its members. As a formal stakeholder, that makes you inherently interested in improving the performance of the plan, which goes back to helping bend the curve with the other programs.

The primary benefit to belonging to a captive is the return on your investment. When the membership base has a good year – where the claims are substantially lower than the investment – the members benefit with a return on their investment typically with the following options:

- **Lower stop-loss premiums**: Premiums reduce upon both the collective performance of the entire captive AND the individual member's performance. If the captive has a good year AND the individual company has a good year, the cost of participation should be beneficial. If the captive does well and the company's performance is marginal, there still may be financial benefits due to the affiliation of participants in the captive.

- **Dividends**: When a captive does well financially, members tend to benefit from dividends that are paid out according to their contributions to the captive's performance. The better a member performs and contributes to the bottom-line performance of the captive, the higher the financial reward. It becomes an opportunity to capture a sizeable reward for the company to add to the reserve to offset future costs.

- **Smooth Cash Flow Impact**: Even when times are a bit rough for a company, and those years happen, participation in a captive can help to smooth out the financial impact. Typically, one bad year can throw premiums into a spin under standard conditions with an employer. One bout of cancer, a car accident, or an expensive transplant can result in years of extended premium increases under typical stop-loss scenarios. In a captive, individual circumstances can affect outcomes, and a member may be assessed higher rates for a specific condition under limited scenarios without continued impact.

Not all captives are created equal. Some are large with hundreds of members to spread the risk. Others are small and tightly controlled to control the risk. Broker fees and commissions may be built in throughout the plans, so be sure you know how those are created. However, if you are looking for additional options to be creative and potentially save money – or even find a return on your costs should you have a particularly good year of claims or several years over time – this may be a solution.

Chronic Disease / Targeted Condition Programs

As you mine data and come to understand the specific challenges that you face as a population, it may become apparent that you have specific conditions that can be addressed with a program. Offering one or more "point solutions" with high-tech, high touch programs designed to help members with specific health issues may provide specific solutions that give members the additional resources they need to address specific conditions.

A targeted program for people with diabetes, for example, may offer both coaching and an interactive glucose monitor that can transmit data to a provider. You may evaluate success by improvement in the quality of life and fewer trips to the emergency room.

Diabetes Management Program

We rolled out a program to address diabetes that integrated both its medical and pharmacy management services. The goal of the plan was to incentivize members to take the necessary steps to control and mitigate the condition through proper treatment. As they followed prescribed treatment regimens, they receive free supplies and medication to address their condition.

Specifically, as the member would consistently refill their prescription, meet with their healthcare provider annually, and attend nutrition and specialist visits, the plan covered **all costs** associated with insulin, testing, and supplies associated with diabetes. The goal was to remove all barriers that might prevent a covered member from complying with prescribed regimens that would keep them healthy.

By monitoring the data analytics, the company could determine if it was making progress in the cost of claims associated with those individuals with this condition. We were saving so much money that we could cover such a program and provide a nice touch even if it was a neutral expense. The more we can do to help those who are contributing to the solution, the better we can make an impact on our goals.

International Mail Order Scripts

Another option for easy cost savings is to provide employees with the opportunity to order medications directly from the manufacturers through international sourcing. Their prescription medications arrive directly to employees' homes in 90-day supplies at no cost to the employees.

We use an option through a group called PetraRx. There may be others available to you. Here's how it works.

The international sourcing allows you to skip the "middleman" price increases that are attached to the pricing of the medications. The overall costs are typically 50% of what they would be through my contracted plan through my carrier, so I save money as the employer. With this cost savings, I waive the copay for employees (on the PPO plan).

Employees receive "free" meds. The employer receives the meds at half of what they were paying for them as a prescription (or even less in many cases). It seems like a win-win so far. By the end of the first year, we had saved tens of thousands of dollars with only a few people taking advantage of it. The program is growing and continues to expand the cost savings.

You can find alternative options. Yes…you have mail order options available to you through your standard plans. Those are great options available that can save you money and you should be promoting them (e.g., ordering 90-day supplies through mail order for a reduced price to the members). That is a significant first step. This program is different and is typically an add-on - a "bolt-on" program…outside of your standard pharmacy benefits management (PBM) program.

It may be worth reviewing.

Direct Primary Care / Onsite or Near-Site Clinics

Addressing Chronic Conditions

With over 150 million Americans reporting one or more chronic condition (driving 90% of US healthcare costs), patients with chronic conditions can benefit from ongoing care. Unfortunately, challenges exist to provide quality care for these individuals, such as:

- **Availability of Care Providers**
  It is becoming more difficult for patients to find available doctors and healthcare professionals to whom they can report. Providing a convenient onsite or near-site option with priority access to employees can increase availability to healthcare that may not otherwise exist to manage ongoing conditions.

- **Convenience of Care**
  Most healthcare providers have designated hours that are only available during the workday, thereby requiring employees to take off work to see their doctor. This inconvenience may also require travel across town and increase the amount of time away from work. An onsite or near-site clinic can reduce or eliminate the need to miss work, thereby limiting the impact on productivity.

- **Consultation and Continuity of Care**
  Onsite or near-site care may provide the opportunity for employees to develop an ongoing regimen of care that builds trust with the doctor that may not currently exist. Regular visits with the same provider may create a stronger rapport that can then influence better care and accountability to support the treatment and improvement of the chronic condition.

Providing convenience-based care management programs to address chronic conditions can be useful to provide care and access but require substantial and sustained engagement from employers to maintain ongoing support from employees.

This approach makes sense IF you have the volume of employees to generate enough savings to justify the overhead. Each business is

151

different, and company size may vary from as few as 1,000 for an on-site provider to make sense. Depending upon the company type, employee demographics, and whether you might facilitate dependent care at your workplace are other considerations.

Onsite Clinics

Onsite clinics are settings where employers offer one or more medical or wellness service, delivered by providers (licensed) to all or a designated group of employees, dependents or others typically on the company's premises. This model is designed to provide easy access at a lower cost to your employees and their families. Employers may incentivize employees with lower costs (or no costs…yes, "free" healthcare) to use the facilities rather than outside physicians or services. Employers use these facilities to control costs and offer these services with far lower overhead than what they pay through traditional healthcare providers paid through their carriers and TPAs. They tend to be a win-win scenario in terms of price, convenience, and service.

The ability to offer onsite services makes sense when an employer is big enough and can cover the overhead for the facility, medical personnel, additional insurance, healthcare related supplies, and costs. The ability to treat common conditions, chronic conditions, provide convenience, and deliver cost-effective healthcare makes sense. Doing so at the right price point is what makes it all work.

The exact number of employees and lives covered is in question – when does it make sense to bring on an onsite clinic? The ROI may take 1000 or more employees before it makes sense. For that reason, most employers cannot make the numbers work. In other cases, they may not want to take on the issues of privacy with health care information, liability insurance, additional overhead in employing physicians, catering to non-employees (e.g., spouses and dependents), etc.

Onsite clinics have been proven to reduce costs by providing affordable healthcare to employees at the place of employment. The idea is that if you can control the costs of overhead and directly providing the services to the employees, thereby skipping the "middleman." It makes sense in many cases. However, many times, employers cannot make the numbers work.

Near-Site Clinics

Smaller employers may not have the resources to host a clinic on-site at their location. Another option may be a near-site clinic – typically established as a clinic used by *multiple* like-minded employers to provide healthcare benefits to their employees. Employers may locate this kind of clinic near the employer's facility (or employers if multiple), giving access to the employees and family members.

This location provides:

- **Access**: With fewer healthcare providers available and growing wait times, a near-site clinic offers additional access to healthcare (and faster access) that may be otherwise unavailable to employees and their families.

- **Convenience**: Locating the clinic near the employer provides greater convenience for employees to run to the doctor for simple conditions and spending less time away from work. It also creates greater convenience for employees and their families to require less travel time to see the doctor. When expanding the services to include employer healthcare such as pre-employment testing, DOT physicals, workers compensation evaluations, etc., employers can maximize the services offered by near-site clinics beyond simple healthcare management.

- **Individual Savings**: Employers can incentivize individuals to use the near site clinic with lower price points such as reduced or no co-pays at the point of service. Like the incentives to use telemedicine, employers can use those same incentives to attract employees to utilize the near site clinic services.

- **Plan Savings**: Employers can have direct control over the cost of providing services. Near-site clinics can directly prescribe generic medicines and perform many of the same tests and labs performed elsewhere. Performing these directly within the near site clinics can save considerable amounts over the cost of other providers.

- **Quality**: Employers also have direct control over the quality of care, which may range from the quality of the services provided to the individuals hired or contracted to provide the care.

- **Greater Privacy**: Offering a near-site clinic instead of an on-site clinic provides greater privacy to individuals. Attending medical treatment on-site may feel awkward if employees sense that others are watching them. Near-site clinics offer a greater sense of privacy to attend to their healthcare needs.

- **Ability to Expand**: Depending upon the success of the venture, a near-site clinic is external. You can expand services either at the location or by finding a separate location if needed.

Third-Party Providers

The thought of directly employing doctors, nurses, and other healthcare providers or owning patient medical records may keep any HR professional up at night. However, the idea of creating a designated location with direct contracting abilities at a cost-effective price is still attractive to any employer as well.

Several groups exist that are willing to establish a designated clinic with direct contracting relationships. These groups are typically set up in a nearby hospital or clinic and will develop a direct contract with you as an employer with the preferred pricing option. As you send your employees and their families to their location and use their services, you can still benefit from an attractive pricing model.

While you will not have direct control over the types of care or quality of care, you may have some control over the cost and range of services. Third party providers may be a viable option if you are not ready to take the plunge into on-site or near-site clinics.

Telemedicine and Telehealth

This idea doesn't necessarily fall into the "cutting edge" side of things given the prevalence of its availability. However, let's talk about how to build it into your strategy to earn the biggest bang for your buck. Let's also talk about the opportunities for this to expand into your plan to improve care and lower costs.

Telemedicine allows employees to access care virtually. This virtual access then enables healthcare professionals to assess, diagnose, and treat patients via the Internet, telephone, etc. While the early stages of telemedicine were clunky at best, we have had some great successes throughout the years. For example, different variations of the Nurse Hotline have been very successful for decades. Allowing a parent to call the nurse at 2 AM about their kids to treat a fever rather than having them rush into the emergency room has saved lives (let alone collectively millions of dollars in medical care).

As the Internet has evolved, so too has our ability to access health and medical care. Generally speaking, "telehealth" includes a broad range of technologies and services to provide patient care and improve the overall healthcare delivery system. It refers to a broader scope of remote healthcare services than telemedicine including nonclinical services, training, and education. These are essential support mechanisms that can help promote healthy living. With online learning, this can provide an integrated support mechanism to help employees and their dependents learn how to improve their abilities to live better.

Telemedicine involves the use of electronic communications – such as the computer, cell phone, telephone, etc. – to provide clinical services without an in-person visit. While telemedicine is useful for follow-up visits, management of chronic conditions, medication management, specialty consultation, and other clinical services, it can also work as an initial visit for simple ailments such as common colds or recurring conditions.

Value to an Employer

Let's talk about the ROI of telemedicine for you as the employer. Here are a few considerations:

155

- **Lower Cost**: Because there is no overhead to the doctor's office, there are substantial savings to providing the service. It is not uncommon for the total cost of a telemedicine physician visit to be $45 compared to a negotiated price for a doctor's appointment of $145.

- **Ease of Access**: If an employee has a computer or a cell phone, they can access the doctor. Sure, there may be the occasional employee who does not feel comfortable using the technology. We cannot avoid offering new technologies to cater to the lowest common denominator. Instead, we should think in terms of how many people can benefit from this convenient option.

- **Quality of Care**: Most telemedicine contracts work in conjunction with medical insurance. Employers should check with the insurance to establish quality control features. In most cases, quality of care is assured.

- **Speed of Care**: Employees and dependents can access real doctors in minutes from the time that they put in their request to have a visit. Doctors are contracted around the country to jump in and visit with patients within minutes. Rather than hoping for a same-day appointment, patients can typically have the appointment completed within minutes of initiation.

- **Reduced Time Loss**: Providing telemedicine options allows employees to access health care faster, thereby reducing the time to seek medical support needed to improve their health. Ultimately, this has the potential to reduce the amount of time away from work.

Value to an Employee

If employees cannot answer the question, "What's in it for me?", it will be a hard sell to pitch something like telemedicine. Here are a few considerations for employees and what's in it for them:

- **Access**: A surprising figure emerges periodically about the number of employees who do not have a designated primary care physician. Much of this stems from their inability to find a physician who is taking on new patients. As such, when an employee is sick, they do not have a doctor to whom they can call and receive immediate attention. Having an option such as telemedicine provides access that they need for prompt attention.

- **Speed of Care**: Having access to medical care in minutes rather than days is enormous. With the reduction of access to physicians, it could take a long time to see the doctor, even if you are sick now. Telemedicine gives you access in just minutes to visit with a healthcare provider.

- **Cost**: Ultimately, the cost of access is up to you as the employer. Whatever the baseline cost is, it is up to you to determine how much you will subsidize it. The level of subsidy will affect your ability to promote utilization. Because we had saved so much in the first two years of our program, and our desire to continue to increase the savings, we made access to telemedicine FREE. We thought that free might be a pretty good price as an incentive to try it out.

- **Privacy**: People generally do not like running into people they know what they go to the doctor. They are not in their best mood or form. Providing telemedicine as an option allows them to maintain additional privacy from the comfort of their home.

- **No Travel / Convenience**: When you are sick, the last thing you want to do is crawl out of bed, get dressed, and go into the doctor's office. With telemedicine, you don't need to do that. You can call in from the comfort of your bed, have a visit with the doctor, and complete with it without hanging out in the doctor's office for two hours waiting for a five-minute conversation to talk about something you already know is wrong with you.

- **Less Time Away from Work**: By providing employees with faster access to the doctor, this can help the treatment start faster and ultimately reduce the employee's time away from work. Sure, the first day away from work may be helpful, but the second day of sitting in bed watching TV becomes old.

Strategies to Bend the Cost Curve

- **Germ-Free**: Staying out of the doctor's office means staying away from all the germs that come with it.

Virtual Behavioral Health

As many as two-thirds of employers provide virtual mental and behavioral health services. Knowing that 1 of every 5 Americans – or over 40 million people – struggle with behavioral health, it makes sense that employers should build in additional resources to help support behavioral health as part of their plan.

There are several virtual solutions to help in delivering those options to employees.

Telephonic Health and Lifestyle Coaching

We have worked with US Wellness Corporation to establish a virtual coaching program for employees in a couple of different categories. First, to assist with our wellness program, we have had a reasonable alternative with weight loss that includes losing 5% of their body weight if they did not meet the BMI standard. While we initially thought this to be a realistic option, at least based upon the research and scientific approach, we also recognize that employees miss the standard regularly.

We brought in US Wellness Corporation to assist us with a different alternative. In addition to the 5% option, we are also providing employees with the opportunity to lose 3% AND complete a six-session coaching program with the health and lifestyle coaches from USWC. The intent is that if we can get the employees to show some effort and demonstrated results through behavior changes while also demonstrating their participation in and successful completion of a program such as health and lifestyle coaching, it makes sense to give them credit for it.

We had tried a virtual option the year before using an online platform, coaches that used an Internet-based approach to communicate through the web and email, and an integrated scale system to engage the participants. We had limited to varied outcomes in that program. It worked in a handful of cases. However, not the results that we were looking for. We switched over to an approach that blends the "human voice" with virtual access to connect our people with real solutions.

159

Coupons

Believe it or not, one of your most effective strategies may be outside of your structured plan altogether. One of the most cost-effective ways to save money may be through a promotional coupon program such as GoodRx.com. There are several programs out there just like it, but I am going to use this one as the example because it is the one with which I am most familiar.

A program such as GoodRx is available to anyone, and you do not need insurance to use it. It is merely a tool to find the best cash price for meds. The great thing about this program is that employees can often find better pricing with cash for their medications than they can with their insurance.

This realization happened just over a year ago as I had this conversation with my doctor. I was taking a medication at the time and as I tried to find the best deals, but at this point with this drug, I had fallen prey to the marketing and read the materials when I picked up my medication from Walgreens. You know, that statement where it says on the prescription bag, "Your insurance saved you $385.00." I thought it was an expensive drug because, for a 30-day supply, my Walgreens statement was telling me this is how much my insurance was covering for me after I was paying my $15 co-pay. When my doctor told me it was a cheap drug, my first thought was, "no… It's a $400 a month drug."

Then we went online.

I entered the medication. I entered my ZIP Code. Then came a list of all the pharmacies in the area, listed by the cost of my prescription for a 90-day supply in CASH. It was just over $20 - FOR A 90-DAY SUPPLY!!!! This had to be a mistake, right?

I went home, looked online at my explanation of benefits, and of course, the marketing was a sham at Walgreens as most things are when it comes to healthcare. It did not cost $400 for that medication. Still, my EOB indicated that the insurance was billing my employer $105 for a 30-day supply of that medication. I was still paying $15 for a 30-day supply that medication. Over the course of 90-days, my employer was paying $315, and I was paying $45 for a total of $360 for a drug that I could receive for the cash price of just over $20. I became ill. It wouldn't be the last time that I felt this way.

I did it again for every medication that my wife and I were taking. By the time I completed this exercise, I was able to reduce our MONTHLY spend by $200, and my company's spend by over $1000.

Cool.

Other programs are out there. For example, promoting the use of Walmart's discount prescription program for cash price meds has always been an excellent opportunity to save money. Other coupon programs exist as well. It's not so much about finding THE right solution as it is getting your employees to identify other alternatives that can help them to engage the entire family in cost-saving solutions.

Strategies to Bend the Cost Curve

SUPPORT STRATEGIES

Support Strategies

With the shifts in mindset in place, let's bring in support strategies that have proven successful with many employers to support and maintain success in their efforts to maintain and reduce healthcare costs. Each organization is different and will require some different support mechanisms to keep the program running smoothly. Depending upon your staff, resources, and energy available to maintain the program, you may need a different set of support mechanisms.

The point of this section is to identify what support strategies you need and plan for them. You may have access to some of these supports early on in your program, and others may take time to develop. Avoid becoming frustrated by not having the entire structure in place from the get-go. This program will take time to develop. Understanding that things will evolve, and needs will change can help you to plan and recognize the need to pivots in certain places along the way as you adjust your plans and your strategies.

Let's consider a few of the support strategies that may be helpful.

Personalized Experiences

There are very few things in this world that are more personal than healthcare. The ability to care for one's kids and family is at the fundamental core of humanity. As an employee comes to work, salary is essential – the ability to pay for the basics of life is the most critical consideration. Just as important these days is the ability to take care of the family's health and well-being – and that is tied directly to the question of health insurance. That becomes personal - which is why the best-run programs are personalized and cater to the specific needs of the individuals.

The best-run programs understand the value of personalizing the individual experience for employees and their dependents. As individuals can design their own experience, they can create an experience that tailors to their needs and provides the best outcomes for their situation.

Programs that allow the individual access to services such as disease management, health assessments, virtual coaching, health advocate services, stress management, lifestyle coaching, and more can meet those needs. However, no matter what you offer within your plan, if the employee does not know that those services exist or how to access them, you may as well not provide them at all.

Health and wellness services assist in the personalized integration of benefits through technology-based resources. Tying in mobile applications, wearables, on-site kiosks, and other web-based resources help to align personal goals and behavior with outcomes. Personalized communications that speak directly to the individuals and their needs are critical to helping them understand.

In our effort to automate functions and processes – which are necessary to keep all the balls in the air with this kind of a program – it is critical to maintaining a level of personalization. Despite your ability to put everything online, avoid canceling your in-person sessions during open enrollment to provide a little bit of handholding for employees and their spouses (yes – invite the spouses and for those conversations). Even though you WANT to "go green" and put everything in an email about your benefits, you NEED to put something in the mail, so the spouse can

166

SEE and TOUCH the information of how to access the steps to answer their healthcare questions.

The desire to automate is excellent. It would be best if you did it to the best of your ability. That is not the point of offering benefits. We are automating to allow us more time to spend with the individual employees and provide them with the experience upon which they may rely.

For example, as we recently switched carriers there was bound to be a hiccup. I had an employee who went to fill an important prescription for his kid. The pharmacist created panic for him and his family by telling him that his kids' medicine was not covered by our insurance any longer. At that moment, that employee no longer cared how much I saved the plan last year. He didn't care how much I dropped his premiums for the coming year. He didn't care about anything that I wrote in this book. All he cared about was in that moment; the pharmacist told him that he could not have the drug that would save his kid's life.

Luckily, we were able to alleviate the panic the next day. The drug was covered, we were able to initiate the pre-authorization, and the transition over to the new insurance provider worked out just fine. However, in those long 16 hours between the time that the pharmacist had told him that they could not have the life-saving drug and the time that he came to visit with me, their entire world was upside down. Healthcare became VERY personal to them very quickly, whereas before it just may have been something that was assumed.

At every step, the more personalized we can make the experience, the better the outcomes for everyone.

Data Analytics

Here's your bottom line:

You can't fix what you don't know.

Top-performing organizations understand the role of data when developing the best programs to control costs and deliver high-performance to employees. According to The Society for Human Resource Management (SHRM), 53% of best-performing companies are using data to analyze benefits results. This data may come in the form of multiyear evaluations of claims data or analysis of employee feedback to consider whether initiatives improve employee health and well-being. However, in all cases, data is a central component of evaluating programmatic efficacy.

I have found data and metrics to be invaluable in my efforts to control costs. Third-party data analytics programs such as NavMD provide this kind of analysis by obtaining raw data and running the correlations and analyses.

The Problem with Data
Here's the problem with data - especially the data that you probably have access to:

Data is not information.

Data involves numbers. Information puts the numbers together, correlates it, and presents it in a useful way. The information takes the data and presents it in a way that draws relationships, correlations, and trends. With this information, you can identify problems, create groups, and visualize strategies that can address significant issues.

Your Source of Data
Most plans rely upon data that comes from the carrier. In the case of fully insured plans, there is no other data available. You are writing the check to them, and they are managing the program. There is nothing else to do so take the data (and information if they have it) and do what you

can to identify trends, options and potential solutions that can help you to curb the costs.

If you are self-funded, you may be leaving your data source to your carrier still - typically coming from their annual report to you, which often includes a rich glossy color portfolio with graphs, charts and large pictures but rarely with any "meat" to the content. In these reports, the carrier typically tells you what a great job they are doing for you and how you should be happy that they are working for you on your behalf. The "information" that you receive is *their* interpretation of what the data means.

Am I saying that your carrier is lying to you?

Not necessarily. However, the carriers have a vested interest in keeping you happy. Their interpretation of reality may not be the same as your interpretation of reality when it comes to evaluating your claims. They may have what they considered to be full analytics and tools available to analyze your data. Again, each carrier is different, and their level of transparency differs as well. If you have useful resources and you trust the data and their ability to create helpful information out of that data, fantastic.

Your broker may also assist in creating useful information and data analysis out of your claims information. With the information provided by the carrier, the broker may take it to the next step and run analyses, trend reports, correlations and make overall recommendations for plan design based upon chronic conditions and most probable value given your population. That is what brokers want to do. However, fewer than 20% will even come close to that level of analysis, especially doing it proactively for you.

For the rest of us...

I strongly recommend the use of outside third-party data resources that can access the raw data from your carriers, extrapolate it, and create reports that identify trends, correlations, and useful information to assist you in managing your plan. I mentioned NavMD because that is the program that I used. I know there are several out there in the marketplace - this is just one.

Strategies to Bend the Cost Curve

Where this practice of using a third-party comes in handy is when you have carved out your pharmacy from your medical. It also helps when you have other ancillary programs as I have described in this book, such as international mail order for drugs. In those cases, and with the help of your brokers, effective reporting through the third party can take those additional costs into account for analysis. This practice can create useful information in terms of trends, chronic conditions, treatments, and total costs of treatment considering ALL expenditures.

Nutritional Counseling

Almost all employers who claim to have a wellness program include an element of nutrition and weight as part of their program. It would make sense that nutrition becomes a part of the conversation. However, when we consider the element of nutritional counseling, only a handful of wellness programs build in formal nutritional counseling into the structure. Whether it includes registered dietitians, nutrition counselors, or simple lunch and learns about the benefits of proper nutrition, the inclusion of the nutritional conversation can enhance the outcomes of your wellness program by focusing on the core building block of its success.

When it comes down to it, food is the fundamental building block of health. You remember what mom said: You are what you eat. There is truth to that. Nutritional counseling focuses on improving the quality of what we are putting into our bodies and using as the fundamental building block of everything else.

Employees can gain from the benefits of a proper diet and healthy lifestyle. Healthful eating patterns can promote weight loss, decrease the prevalence of diabetes, increased sports performance, speed healing time from injuries, and so much more. With a little bit of support and guidance, employees can build eating plants that fit their lifestyle and food preferences, which then help them to go the extra mile to help them lead healthier and more fulfilling lives.

This fundamental change can affect everything from how they feel, energy level, attitude, anxiety and depression, inflammation, and more. Chronic conditions such as diabetes, abnormal blood sugar, high cholesterol, eating disorders, and metabolic disorders can all be controlled more effectively when the nutritional balance is right.

As an employer, doesn't this make sense? When you think about the benefits of these outcomes, you start talking about lower absenteeism, higher engagement, fewer accidents and injuries, lower prescription costs, higher morale, lower turnover, higher performance - and the list continues.

Ideas for Including Nutritional Counseling

How you build your nutritional counseling program will depend upon your structure, program, and population. There are several variations of resources available to you. Taking a one-size-fits-all approach never works but offering 100 options when only ten are needed does not make sense either. Consider some of these options when developing nutritional counseling for your employees.

- **Lunch and Learn Events**
  Offering 30- to 45-minute lunch and learn events is a quick and easy way to promote services and educational options to employees. Employees can bring their lunch, sit down and listen, and learn something new. If you have points available to earn through your incentive program, offering a few points can't hurt to motivate attendance. It is typically easy to find a local vendor who will present for free. On occasion, they may even be willing to bring lunch.

- **One-on-One Nutritional Counseling Services**
  In some cases, you may offer nutritional counseling under your insurance plan. If this is the case, you may find a provider to come in to deliver services on-site under the plan guidelines. If not, you can promote the use of nutritional counseling services as it makes sense.

- **Chronic Condition Specific Nutritional Counseling**
  There may be chronic conditions that can benefit from specific nutritional counseling. For example, controlling Type-II diabetes would be a perfect example of using nutritional counseling to target specific conditions.

- **Nutritional Seminars**
  Like lunch and learns, additional seminars may be explicitly provided to nutrition and health.

- **Cooking Classes**
  Several companies offer an after-hours cooking course for employees and their spouses. They may sponsor a well-known chef to provide a class on healthy cooking. Third parties are available to you may also sponsor these.

172

- **Nutrition Coaches**
  Some employers bring coaches on site as another way to assist employees and provide resources to them. Employees can visit with nutrition coaches to set menus, discuss eating options, and find ways to match nutritional requirements with eating preferences to meet their goals.

- **Posters**
  As with any campaign, a well-designed and well-placed poster can help reinforce your message. Knowing what you want to say and how to say it, you can share critical nutritional messaging throughout the workplace.

- **Guide to Losing Weight**
  There are several resources in the marketplace that provide free "guides" to losing weight using proper nutrition. The CDC offers several resources. Several county health departments have their own, which may be an excellent resource.

- **Access to Healthy Foods**
  Several employers offer food through vending machines or a company store, which is often the source of lunch, snacks, or a steady stream of caloric intake among employees. Finding an opportunity to place healthy food options in those locations is excellent. However, if those options are heavily subsidized and far less expensive than their sugary counterparts, they may start to look attractive.

- **Healthy Foods at Meetings**
  Skipping the donuts and bringing the apples may be your best bet if you want to promote healthy lifestyle changes and set the tone for a culture of wellness.

- **Water as the Default Beverage**
  It's cheaper, easy, and healthy.

- **Access to Commercially Available Nutrition Programs**
  Several programs exist that can be offered in the workplace if there is enough interest. For example, an employer may choose

to offer Weight Watchers at work. This option may run from merely finding a room and letting employees pay for the full fee to heavily subsidizing their program costs.

- **Apps**
  Promoting wellness tools and resources through company-sponsored apps may help to drive engagement and support for your programs.

Lunch and Learns

While I have mentioned lunch and learns before, I list this out as a separate support structure because of their efficacy. Lunch and learns provide a way to bring in somebody from the "outside" share best practices, good ideas, and helpful hints with employees.

While the focus of this book is health and wellness, we use lunch and learns for the broad range of wellness, including financial wellness. Our primary delivery source of financial wellness topics is through lunch and learns. We have not had an issue with finding local companies willing to bring in a representative to speak on a topic that makes sense under our wellness program. In many cases, the speakers may come from our vendors and provide reliable resources specific to a plan that we currently offer. In other cases, they may be local vendors, and the quid pro quo is simple exposure to our employees.

While attendance will vary depending upon the topic and your employee base, we offer incentives to our employees to attend. By attending, employees can earn a few points that go to their wellness incentives. Those wellness incentives then contribute to the overall value received as they earn HSA incentives.

Topics for lunch and learns have included subject matter such as:

- **Personal Budgets**: Financial Planner – How to set starter budgets or use the budgeting system to improve your financial security.

- **Starting an Exercise Program**: On-site Personal Trainer – Designed for those who have not built an exercise program in the past but want to start somewhere.

- **Tax Preparations**: A local manager from H&R Block sharing the latest updates in the tax code and what employees need to know before they file their taxes.

- **Healthful Eating**: Nutritionist from local business explaining the essential elements involved with healthy eating.

175

- **Stress Reduction for the Holidays**: Behavioral Counselor sharing best practices of ways to reduce personal stress during the holiday season. (This was offered just after Thanksgiving)

- **Mindfulness**: Clinical Behavioral Specialist - With all the stresses and pressures of life, it is critical to find opportunities to be mindful of where we are in the present time and with whom we are spending our time.

- **Improving Your Credit Score**: Credit Union Representative presents ten ways to improve credit ratings to prepare for purchasing homes, cars, and other items.

Our objective is to have a lunch and learn about every 1 to 2 months to bring in fresh ideas, offer new opportunities to learn and to gain exposure to the outside talent that may allow us new ideas and perspectives. Not only does this provide education, but it also increases engagement, interaction, and facetime with employees as you seek to build relations of trust with them.

Weight Management Programs

Let's get to the point.

Weight is the #1 driver of cost in your plan.

Weight (especially obesity) affect every company in the United States. On average, at least a third of your employees are overweight, and another third are obese. It is a "big deal" when you consider what comes with these conditions...

- Heart Disease and Stroke

- High Blood Pressure

- Diabetes

- Liver Disease

- Cancer

- Osteoarthritis, Joint Disease

- Gout

- Breathing Problems

- Gallbladder Disease and Gallstones

Unless your top claim is genetic or accidental, there's an excellent chance that your top trends are related to poor health that relate to one or more of these conditions.

The latest from the Center for Disease Control and Prevention claims that seven out of every ten deaths among Americans each year come from chronic diseases such as heart disease, cancer and diabetes stemming from PREVENTABLE conditions (data from cdc.gov). Along

177

the same lines, these same conditions account for 75% of the nation's health spending. These chronic conditions can be largely preventable!!!

In 2018, there were 2.2 million related hospitalizations and 415,000 deaths specific to heart attacks and strokes alone (data from aarp.org). The worst part? At least 80% of those are estimated to have been preventable with lifestyle adjustments, relatively inexpensive and available medications, and a shift in attitude.

Look…if you knew something was going to kill you, wouldn't you do what you could to stop it? Or avoid it?

A speeding bus is headed right at you…and you're standing right in the middle of the road. The bus isn't stopping. Wouldn't you try to do something to get out of the way? As the employer, wouldn't you want to do something to coax your employee to step out of the way? As a fellow human, you should want to help. As the fiscal agent who will be responsible for paying for the damage that will ensue after this collision, you should have a vested interest in WANTING to help prevent this wreck from happening.

Guess what? Eating healthy, exercising regularly, avoiding tobacco, and accessing preventable services are all ways that we can do what it takes to prevent the bad and promote the good. It takes more than merely offering the occasional "Biggest Loser" competition and dumping a few pounds.

Why the Employer Influences the Most
Understand this…people spend more waking hours at work than anywhere else!

Employees spend more hours at work with their coworkers than they do with their spouses, kids, friends, and family members during any given week. You have more influence – for good or otherwise – over their lives than anyone else.

It takes a commitment as the employer to make a positive influence in the lives of your employees. With this influence, you can make a positive influence that can change lives that will last a lifetime. Remember…it's not about saving money on claims. It's about making permanent changes.

Saving money is the outcome of doing the right thing for your people. Saving lives is the outcome of putting the right programs in place that affect people at the core that can help them to live longer, better lives.

Goals of Your Weight Management Program

Just like the diversity of your employee group, your weight management program must have different approaches. You have different needs and conditions to be addressed. Diverse interests and education levels will determine what will work and what won't. Some members will just need a little "nudge" to get going while others may need more to get things going.

At the same time, remember the three groups. Unless you are the anomaly, no matter what you do, you'll never get 100% buy-in for this program. The top 25% will be supportive and early adopters. The middle 50% will generally go the direction of the loudest voice (so you MUST be the most booming voice along with the adopters). The bottom 25% will be the resistors and fight you every step of the way. Stop worrying about trying to win the bottom 25% - instead, continue to win and love your top 25% who will then influence your middle 50%. That is where your goals should focus.

Consider these goals of your weight management programs:

- **Member Engagement**
  Engagement is proactive. It sets up the tools for success, provides guidelines, establishes parameters, and creates a rewards structure that is easy to follow. It is also easy to generate excitement. As employees understand the program, identify the answer to the fundamental question of "what's in it for me" and then go after the incentives, they will drive the program for you. You must get out of the way for it to happen.

- **Reduce Current Risk**
  You are almost guaranteed to have considerable risk in your population right now. Anything you can do to reduce that is a priority. Just remember that we want to do it the right way and avoid actions that will cause even more significant harm in the short run or the long term. Offering a program over eight-weeks with a substantial prize at the end provides a more common-sense approach to weight loss over two-weeks.

179

- **Prevent Future Risk**
  It's not enough to take the weight off. We also want to keep it off. In some competitions, I have seen cases where the same individuals will win time and time again. They take the initial weight off, put it back on, and then take it back off the next time around. Finding opportunities to reward or incent carry-over or long-term positive behavior is advantageous. For example, we started to offer several bonus points in our competitions when participants weighed in within 1% or lower of their previous weight from the last competition if they competed. This incentive sent the message clearly that it's not just about the weight loss for <u>this</u> program, but we are promoting healthy living.

- **Promote Wellness**
  Your weight loss competition should also incorporate elements of wellness. Bringing in fun competitions in conjunction with the weight loss challenge helps to engage employees and enhance the fun aspect of the event. For example, weekly "walk-offs" involving step competitions at the individual or team levels may add additional opportunities for camaraderie.

The more engaging and fun the program, the more likely it is to succeed. People don't want to hear the answer to the question, "How do I lose weight?" They already know the answer - eat less, exercise more. They're looking for support and solutions to help them get further down the path.

Ideas to Start the Conversation and Engage
There are several tools, resources, and support systems available to employers as they launch weight management programs. Many of these programs have been around for years, while others are relatively new to the market. The key is to be aware of what these tools and resources are and how they may tie to your program. While the following is a limited list, it may be the starting point for you to begin your research and dialogue with others to find the right tools that can work for you and your employees.

- **Body Scanning**

Using the standard scale is great...and if you do, be sure you use a high-quality scale. Use one that will be digitally accurate and consistent each time. This accuracy will require you to spend more than just 35 bucks on a bathroom scale.

We have had great success in using body scanning scales that do a total body composition for employees which helps them get a complete baseline of where they are at with body mass index, total fat, total muscle, and other metrics. I have used this at multiple employers. Using body comp scanners is not intended to collect data but rather to provide a service to the employees, so they understand not just weight, but also the composition of fat and muscle. When they begin to understand the total picture – not only weights – they can know where they are at and where to improve. I tend to favor the total body composition scales by Tanita. They are expensive, but I see them as an investment.

Other mobile scanning technology is becoming available to bring onsite assistance to employees for cardiac, pulmonary, and other health evaluation services. New 3D scanning technology is impressive and may prove even more valuable for employer investment in the future.

- **Weight Loss / Maintenance Challenges**
  Most workplaces run some kind of "Biggest Loser" challenge. They tend to be fun, easy, and straight forward. These are great ways to create momentum, excitement, and engagement among employees. Building camaraderie when it comes to employee wellness is the best way to build momentum.

When we first started, we only focused on weight LOSS competition. As we offered points tied to incentives, the wellness platform (which then tied into HSA contributions), and other offers, our healthy population – whom we are trying to keep healthy and motivated – started to complain a bit about not the same love. So we included them in the competitions from a "maintenance" perspective to help drive additional engagement and energy throughout the workplace.

I have found that the most effective workplace weight competitions include the following elements:

181

○ **Teams**: Don't forget the power of the team! The ability to get to the desired outcomes depends upon the support received. Bringing in teams, offering special incentives such as additional points, tying in extra rewards, and engaging groups is a great way to take your weight loss challenges to the next level.

○ **Healthy Weight Loss**: Promoting healthy weight loss options is essential. This effort requires weight loss competitions to stretch over a reasonable time, such as eight weeks or 12 weeks. Promoting crash diets over the course of four weeks or less is unhealthy. It is also unsustainable as people will put that weight back on that they quickly took off.

○ **Avoid Overload**: I have found that running one well-planned weight loss challenge per year is far more effective than running two or three competitions that seem rushed. Employees tend to have "weight loss overload" if too many competitions emerge in a year. Our perfect balance has seemed to be one weight loss competition in the spring and one "maintain, don't gain" campaign during the holidays.

○ **Substantial Rewards**: Having a significant award for the winner is great. However, we also offer substantial rewards for those who participate actively throughout the entire campaign. We tie them to activity points connected to the wellness platform, which link to incentives. Offering enough points to make it worth their while is key to engaging employees and creating the motivation to change behavior.

○ **Intermittent Rewards for Participation**: We also found the opportunity to engage employees by offering points for intermittent weigh-ins. If it is an eight-week weight loss challenge, we provide points for weigh-ins every two weeks. Rather than merely waiting until the end and hoping for the best, we continuously engage employees by having mid-competition weigh-ins. Sure,

it takes additional time to weigh people. However, we
have interns to help with that, and it gives us another
opportunity to engage with employees.

- o **Incorporate Education**: Providing educational elements
  via email, lunch and learns, and other opportunities to
  enhance the healthy living aspect is essential to
  increased engagement.

- **Mileage/Walking/Steps Competitions**
  If you have a wellness platform, chances are good it already
  allows individual wearable fitness trackers to connect and track
  activities. If not, you may sponsor programs through third parties
  to enable employees to connect their devices and join a steps
  competition. Using a central platform allows employees to
  register automatically, allows you to automate the competition,
  provides third-party assistance to track progress, and facilitates
  the fun.

- **Food Sources**
  If you have a company store or vending machines and all they
  offer are white sugar, gluten, and empty calories, the employees
  will pick up on that very quickly. You don't have to replace
  everything. However, finding healthy options to offer employees
  is helpful.

  That said, most employers who try this give me the feedback that
  when they do, those products don't sell. An apple next to a
  Snickers bar does not stand a chance. However, what if the apple
  were free? Or only $0.10? Would that change the attitude about
  the choice of the apple? We may have more opportunity to
  influence food choices than we think.

- **Bariatric Resources**
  For some of you, you may be ready for the conversation of
  bariatric surgery. I am a huge advocate for healthy eating,
  lifestyle management, time in the gym, and the other approaches
  to managing health and well-being. Cutting your way to a
  thinner body is not the first alternative (nor should it ever be).

However, as I will share next after you try the alternatives, genetics may be working against you. Bariatrics may be a viable solution to assist in helping employees achieve their wellness goals. It is not for everyone, and I am not advocating for it as a solution for everyone. It may be a solution for you to consider as part of the weight loss conversation.

Wade's Journey

I share the following in case someone else is struggling. This is not meant to be a "hey, look at me" kind of a story. Instead, perhaps it's reflective of someone's journey who you know and this may provide some assistance.

I admit. Mine has been a challenging journey that has been with me for life. As a kid, I suffered from childhood obesity. It was in my genes. We came from sturdy Nordic stock. My siblings, cousins, parents, aunts, uncles, grandparents…everyone…suffered from what my Uncle Vern called the "Dunlop Disease." My belly had "done lopped" over my belt, much like the rest of the family.

There was a brief time in high school where I was active and participated in sports. I ran during the summers, did football in the fall, track in the spring (shotput and discus), and was generally active so I was able to keep the weight off through much of my high school years and until I was about 21.

Then came the stresses of life. College, marriage, kids, poor sleeping habits, poor diet, and everything else that comes with the territory hit all at once. My 169 lb. marriage weight skyrocketed. What I didn't realize at the time – and wouldn't for another decade – was that my thyroid would be slipping into hypothyroidism. What I wouldn't understand for another 25 years was that I was also insulin resistant. I knew my family was prone to diabetes – both parents, both sets of grandparents, aunts, uncles, etc. all had it. I was trying to dodge it, but the weight kept on stacking on.

As I was fighting my own battle, I knew the wellness challenge – we needed wellness as an employer, and I needed to be the one to build it at first. However, I also was the one that needed it the most.

184

The first time I built the program was at North Idaho College. I've shared the story in bits and pieces through the book, but it comes across as a bit of a hypocrite as I promote wellness while I am looking like the antithesis of the very program I am promoting. Admittedly, it was a challenge, and I knew it. Still, we built it, I participated in it, but nothing was happening despite my best efforts.

Through these years, I tried every program out there. If it promised weight loss, I tried it - probably twice or three times. I also worked out in the gym. As a former high school athlete, I knew what it took to get in shape and I did it regularly, but without results. It was frustrating to get into a standard regimen only to fail at seeing anything beyond minimal effects time after time.

I recognized the signs. Lethargy. Snoring (my poor wife!). Anxiety – followed by depression (they're both just opposite ends of the same spectrum). It was crazy!

Here I was again in my career, doing it a second time. With great success the first time around, saving the college millions of dollars through its wellness-based program, another company is looking for the same kind of solution. However, the stakes are higher this time around. Rather than a proactive solution, we are facing a desperate situation. I was coming into the organization as a true outsider, asking people to change their ways fundamentally and to do so in short order. The system was failing and failing fast - without a fast turnaround, we were looking at massive increases for the company and employees for years to come.

I knew wellness was at the heart of it all, but again – here's this severely obese so-called "expert" in wellness trying to schlep culture change for a program that on the outside looks like he doesn't live himself. Why should anyone follow him if he doesn't support it himself? It's a real challenge – not just a situation of self-imposed doubts and fears.

At this point, we move forward. I have no other choice and we have success. About a year into the new program, my doctor has a real conversation with me – one that is unlike any other I've had with past doctors. Rather than simply telling me that I should "eat less and exercise more," she asks me questions.

The first question - how long have you been insulin resistant?

185

Strategies to Bend the Cost Curve

Hmm...I don't know what that means. She told me I was pre-diabetic. That news was shocking and held my attention. I had tried so hard to avoid that news, and here it was staring right at me. I was diabetic (or pre-diabetic). My *fear of needles* was facing me. But insulin resistance? She explained that the pancreas was producing insulin - it was producing 30-50 TIMES the average amount that it should because the receptors were not absorbing it. The body told the pancreas to produce it, but then couldn't receive it which generated the desire to eat...and eat hard (sugar, carbs, all the bad stuff). That drove the cycle to get me where I was.

First thing's first - control the madness with medication. And we did.

A year went by, and while I didn't gain any more, I didn't lose any either. It was time for the doctor to go to the next question that would have the most significant impact on me.

Second question - how do you sleep?

I sleep fine. I've never had a problem sleeping. I'm pretty much narcoleptic as I can fall asleep anywhere at any time. I slept the number of hours I had available.

Here's the BONUS question that NO ONE had asked me before...How do you FEEL when you wake up?

This question was life changing. I told her that I usually felt more tired than when I went to sleep. I didn't suffer from nightmares but had VERY active dreams. She was able to prescribe a medication that helped me to get into 3rd stage REM...which I had never hit before. While I slept, I never had the rest I needed because my mind never let me get into the full REM cycle.

The next morning, I turned to my wife and asked, "Is this how you feel when you wake up?" Never in my life had I felt refreshed when I woke up. EVER. Once rested, I could control my food addictions, resolved my anxiety, and improved my attitude.

She also introduced me to an eating plan specific to insulin-resistant patients. I never went hungry and followed the plan. Wow. (Again, I don't mind passing along what worked. Feel free to look up Jorge

Cruise's "Belly Fat Cure" books. Awesome!!) I lost 55 pounds over three months and started to feel great.

After a plateau, I had to come to that moment where I asked what to do next. I knew what I had faced for the previous 26 years. Based on my childhood obesity and my genetics, I knew the battle I would be fighting for the rest of my life. I also saw the success my brother and sister had with elective bariatric surgery to help. While I had lost 55 lbs., that was just a dent when your starting point was 332.

I had made great connections with our friends at CIMA Hospital in San Jose, Costa Rica. Given the price difference between having the surgery there vs. the U.S., we chose there. The employer was favorable in trying it out, so they covered the cost of the operation. Off we went.

It's never meant to be a quick fix, but I responded well, and it continued my journey of permanent change. Over the next several months, I dropped an additional 80 lbs. for a total of 135 pounds over the course of a year.

Does it make a difference?

Here's the scary-cool part.

When the surgeon was in there, he looked at my liver. I heard I had a "fatty liver," but no one told me how bad things were. My surgeon let me know his observations were that it was at "stage 4 fatty liver" entering cirrhosis. OK, that grabbed my attention. Even with the changes, I had made the year before, the body was screaming for help. After just a few months post-surgery, my blood tests came back, and my liver enzyme production indicated that the liver had complete healed itself. Incredible.

So, with a new lease on life, I'm committed more now than ever to the message of leading change within the organization in a way that can help people change their lives. It's not about the money. Saving money will happen when we start taking care of what matters most.

On-Site Gym

I've mentioned the story of how the onsite gym came to be at one of my employers. Using the initial cost savings from a successful negotiation (vs. taking the money and running with it) was a great way to make a statement to employees that we were serious about our launch into wellness.

We found a section in the lower level used for storage and remodeled. A basic wall, paint on the walls, TVs with cable, and of course a giant logo for our new wellness program. If you can brand it, you can sell it - and that goes for your wellness program as well.

After careful consideration, we partnered with a local fitness and exercise supplier in town to provide an array of commercial equipment to get us started. We wanted to offer a workout experience just as good as the local gym (no junky stuff!), so we invested in proper equipment.

We set it up with an array of cardio and weights – both universal and free weights – to allow everyone to get what they needed. More importantly, we set it up to be accessible to everyone and to reduce barriers to participate.

Nothing says that you're committed to wellness like setting up an on-site gym, but this is not the first time that we did it. Previously, we had to do it in phases – similarly finding an open space, purchasing the equipment as we could, and building up the facility as we went. Our current model allowed us to buy high-end commercial gear. The previous model allowed us to buy the best that Costco could provide to us. In both cases, it worked.

At this stage, the HR folks are going to ask me questions about liability. Yes, I had them sign waivers to use the gym. No, I did not let the spouses and dependents use it to avoid additional liability. Yes, the liability waiver is intended to waive the Worker's Compensation aspect should they get injured. Will it protect me 100%? I hope so – but there is a risk in everything that we do. Right now, I know that there is a high risk if we do nothing. Offering people a chance to get healthy and providing the tools to get there is a pretty good way to reduce my other risks.

On-Site Trainer and Participatory Classes

Having an on-site gym is excellent. Having an on-site trainer within the gym is even nicer. We saved so much money during the first couple of years of our program that we could afford to bring on an on-site trainer to offer small group classes to our employees during the afternoons.

After the first year of the new gym, it was apparent that some people were using the facilities, but most people were not. The utilization rates were low. We needed a way to get people into the gym to use the facilities and feel comfortable doing so. We contracted with an on-site trainer to begin the process of educating others to use the equipment, take a couple of classes, and provide introductory instruction.

It became evident that there was a higher demand to have workout classes offered to our employee groups. We started with a handful of classes which grew to a full series of the sessions provided in the afternoons, 4-days per week. We are now at the point of having waiting lists for individuals who want to take additional courses. The classes are at no cost to the employees provided they attend ALL the sessions. If they fail to participate in the class, they pay $40 per month.

After several months, it also became evident that we have several exceptional cases that require additional attention. These are high-risk individuals that had requested other services. These additional services include nutritional counseling, personal one-on-one coaching from our trainer, and extra care that they need to set and achieve their personal training goals. We expanded the contract of the on-site trainer to attend to as many as 12 of these individuals at any time.

Over the course of the first year, we had dozens of individuals take advantage of these classes and services. Individual stories of lowering cholesterol, lowering blood pressure, and reducing risk factors emerged. Spending a little extra money on a personal trainer now to help save a heart attack, stroke, or knee replacement in the future makes sense.

Integrated Wellness

Finally, it makes sense for an organization to take an integrated wellness approach, observing ALL areas of wellness – not just the physical side of it.

Following the model provided by the Wellness Council of America (WELCOA), a comprehensive wellness program includes not only physical well-being but also other areas including (www.welcoa.org):

- **Physical**: We have spent considerable time talking about the physical elements of wellness. A healthy body is essential to reducing the claims and the costs associated with your overall healthcare program.

- **Social**: As mentioned before, people spend more waking hours at work and with their coworkers than they do at home with their spouse or children. It is essential that they feel welcome, comfortable, and integrated into the workplace from a social perspective.

- **Intellectual**: The workplace should provide intellectually stimulating opportunities to grow and develop from a personal and professional perspective. Wellness is integrated into these levels as the employer offers plenty of opportunities to grow in those areas.

- **Spiritual**: How an individual feels about his or her presence in an environment matters. This element is not talking about religion in the workplace, but rather how an individual thinks about his or her place in this world. Part of a comprehensive and integrated wellness program is ensuring the overall well-being of the individual and feeling comfortable with who they are and where they are.

- **Emotional**: This goes to the heart of mental and behavioral health, which we have discussed. Ensuring behavioral health is of critical importance to any employer.

- **Occupational**: The ability to grow and develop, all while feeling safe and secure: within one's job is essential. Occupational well-being covers the gamut of all the things we discussed.

190

Other Ideas

As mentioned at the start, this book was never about providing a comprehensive guide in the form of a text. Instead, it was meant to be a resource or a guide of best practices and approaches that have been successful in building programs that works. The ideas and plans laid out in the book are just those – ideas that have worked for me and my organizations. They may or may not work for you depending upon your employees, situation, resources, etc.

There are other tools and resources that I have used successfully that I have not necessarily discussed in the book. There are other resources in use by other organizations as well that are worth mentioning. I have decided to put them into a catch-all group here at the end of "Other Ideas" that are worth mentioning...

- **Behavioral Health / Counseling** – Employers are sensitive to the need to provide for the behavioral health needs of employees. These services may include coverage for psychotherapy and counseling services. Mental and behavioral health inpatient services are just as critical as medical treatment and substance use disorder (i.e., substance abuse) treatment is of growing concern, especially with the opioid crisis facing America. Employers must consider behavioral health resources when developing comprehensive wellness strategies.

  At a minimum, a robust Employee Assistance Program (EAP) is essential. Offering adequate counseling assistance with enough visits to employees and their dependents is an excellent start to providing the help they need when they need it.

- **Stress Reduction Programs** – Stress is the number one cause of depression, anxiety, headaches, insomnia, irritability, and other challenges to individual health. As an organization, stress can lead to higher turnover, lower morale, reduced productivity, higher claims costs, absenteeism, and even workers compensation claims. The causes of stress are varied coming from workload to personal challenges, management style to workplace harassment. A company can implement a variety of stress reduction programs to help alleviate the overall stress and tension to address these everyday ailments. Ideas may include incorporating flexible working schedules, improving communications, increasing recognition, encouraging breaks and relaxation, generating more opportunities to move around, resolving workplace conflicts, training managers to develop relationships and work dynamics, and improving ergonomics are some approaches taken by employers.

- **Value-Based Designs** – Aligning the patients and provider incentives towards efficient care, preventing recurrence of illness, and reducing complications. Descriptions of these programs use bundle payment approaches for medical plans which are a form of contracting using pre-and post-procedural care into one negotiated price. In some ways, this seems to overlap a bit with reference-based pricing and direct contract approaches that we talked about before.

Perhaps another approach to value-based designs is to design your benefits program around what your employees and their dependents need. In many cases, you may have programs and plans that offer far more than what you need. In other cases, you may be underrepresenting the needs of your employees and not providing the care that is essential to take care of them. As we have described, when we don't take care of the employees, and they don't get the care that they need, it could end up costing us far more in the long run.

Here are some considerations when assessing the value of your plan and its design configuration:

- **Bundled Pricing** – Under the heading of "negotiated pricing strategies" is bundled pricing to establish a set price for a procedure wherein all costs are determined up front. This practice prevents the "nickel and diming" that can take place as bills accumulate over weeks and even months and minor procedural statements arrive from multiple sources such as the hospital, doctor, anesthesiologist, nursing support, housekeeping, etc. Setting a single price – up front – means no surprises, one "all in" amount that is agreed to, and establishes a form of managed care that leaves no one shocked or surprised in the end.

This approach allows an employer and a patient to apply consumerism as they shop pricing and compare the total value of cost, quality (via net promoter scores or other metrics), travel options, and other logistics.

- **Emphasize Pharmacy Strategies** – As we mentioned several times, drug expenses will continue to climb, and it doesn't look like this is going to stop anytime soon. Evaluating your spending on expensive specialty drugs such as Biologics that are injected or infused should raise some questions about alternatives and options. As patents expire, generics become available, and more bio-similar start to hit the market, employers should identify opportunities to identify best-performing solutions that still meet quality standards to steer patients away from hospitals and towards a doctor's office or home administration.

- **Case Management** - If you are fully funded, chances are good that your carrier already has case management built-in as they are acutely aware of costs and doing their part to control their spending. If you are self-funded, it is essential that you identify opportunities to manage cases to consider trends, special situations, and opportunities to assist employees and their dependents to obtain the best care possible. Anyone left to navigate the healthcare system on their own will soon feel deserted and frustrated.

  Using a case management process will help to identify barriers that may prevent people from getting the best care possible, navigate challenges, and help find the right solutions. While there may be an additional administrative cost for such a service, the value added will more than pay for it. Merely reducing the time it takes to obtain services, eliminating the need for additional services, and improving the quality of outcomes are just a few of the value-added opportunities that come from effective case management.

  If you currently have case management services but find that they are not providing the service you want or need, keep in mind that there are many third-party options out there that have proven effective — these range from patient advocates to full case managers.

- **Prior Authorization** – Most plans, especially those looking to save a buck, have built-in some form of prior authorization to prevent carte blanche access to expensive procedures. The tighter the prior authorization process, the more barriers that exist for people to overcome to access the care that they need. It's a delicate balance. On the one hand, you want them to get the care that they need so they can get better. On the other hand, you want them to take the necessary steps to get a second opinion and ensure that they are getting the care that they do need.

There are best practices built-in to effective prior authorization steps to ensure that you can make the most out of your prior authorization process such as:

- **Transparency Tool** – Over half of employers offer a price transparency tool to help employees choose the best services or products available to them at the best price. Using transparency tools allow employees to see the real cost of services so they can compare prices from one facility and physician to another. For those individuals who are consumer-minded, they can find new ways to save money when they are working on their deductible, co-insurance, and co-pays.

Proactive employers are finding opportunities to incorporate transparency tools with programs that allow employees to receive cash incentives when they save money using transparency tools. As employees find opportunities to save money for the plan, employers are finding opportunities to take a portion of cost savings and reward employees directly in the form of gift cards, HSA contributions, and cash.

- **Spousal Coverage** - Cost-sensitive employers are seeking ways to reduce costs and the administrative burden of tracking coverage for nonemployees have been found to impose surcharges on spouses who could elect coverage elsewhere. In other words, if the spouse is offered medical insurance at their job, but the employee chooses to cover the spouse under his/her plan, the employer hits them up with a spousal surcharge, typically as much as 40%.

This strategy comes with a heavy pro and con attached. The advantage, of course, is the ability to defer the cost of coverage for the spouse to the other plan. The disadvantage becomes the lack of "friendliness" to the employee. Given the challenge to find and keep talent in the workplace, this may be just one more thing that may be a dissatisfier to your employees.

- **Health Advocacy** – Given the complexity that exists in managing health insurance and medical claims, it makes sense to offer a health advocacy program to employees that provide them the service to give someone a call and help them navigate bill payments and coverage options. I have used the company Health Advocate for years. There are others out there that do a good job as well. By using a health advocacy service, it frees you up in HR while still providing the service to your employees that they need.

- **Offer Incentives for Cost-Effective Procedures or Facilities** – We have addressed this in several ways within this book. However, in case you're jumping to the "punchline" first, let me reiterate the value in offering incentives as the way to motivate behavior change. Remember:

  o That which gets measured gets done...
  o That which gets measured and rewarded improves...
  o That which gets measured, reported and rewarded gets repeated...

  If you want behavior change that sticks, find an incentive that is big enough and valuable enough to adjust behavior. Where practical, find a way to give employees back a portion of the money that they save the plan. For example, if they use a facility that is significantly more cost-effective, offer to waive co-pays, co-insurance, or even offer gift cards, HSA contributions and cash payments as an incentive to use those facilities.

- **Help Employees Develop an Emergency Plan** – The worst thing an employee can do is wait until a crisis hits to figure out what to do for their health care options. When they do, they tend to make poor healthcare decisions (e.g., go to the emergency room for a minor incident). A simple exercise of helping employees to figure out where they would go in the event of an emergency can avoid heavy financial burdens later.

This exercise might include:

- o Identifying where the local Emergency Room is located.
- o Identifying where the closest Urgent Care facility is located.
- o Selecting a primary care provider (PCP) for regular care for themselves and their family member.
- o Educating when it is appropriate to go to which facility.
- o Plans should include telemedicine and how to access services.

- **Tobacco Cessation Programs** – Smoking and tobacco cessation programs are a great way to lower your costs over the long term. When you think about it, this is a no-brainer when you consider the direct impact to cost and negative impact to the user and those around him or her (e.g., second-hand smoke). Combining a cessation program with an effective rewards component increase the odds of employees quitting by three times (vs. just offering the program alone).

- **Centers of Excellence** – I struggled to decide whether to pull this section out as a stand-alone section or whether to keep it as an honorable mention due to its potential for impact to an organization. The concept of a Center of Excellence (COE) is based on cost and quality…its overall value.

The ability to direct an employee to a COE where they specialize in transplants, joint replacements, cardiac or cancer provides some assurance about the quality of care the patient is most likely to receive. If we pay a bit more for the cost of travel for the employee to receive services at a COE, and we pay a bit more for the facility, and we pay a bit more for the expertise of the physicians, but in return we have a track record of fewer complications, faster healing, less infection, higher quality, and other measures, does it make it worthwhile? We may pay more on the front end but may pay less overall when everything is taken into consideration.

- **Lactation Support Services** – As new mothers return to work, it is essential that we provide a comfortable work environment wherein they can be effective at balancing both work and home life. This balance includes the need to maintain their efforts to support natural lactation if that is their choice. From comfortable and private lactation locations to lactation services (including access to lactation specialists and coaches), employers are going all out to do what they can to assist employees.

- **Onsite Health Fairs** - We've addressed this previously, but never underestimate the power of engagement. Providing an opportunity to allow employees and their spouses to engage with insurance carriers and providers of voluntary benefits is useful in helping them to navigate the healthcare wilderness. It also wins brownie points for you as employees can meet new people, identify new opportunities for personal services, and pick up a little swag along the way for fun.

- **Onsite Immunization Clinics** – This is a no-brainer and we're going to list it. Offering immunizations at no-cost is essential to promote a healthy workforce, including free flu shots onsite to ensure cost-effective and convenient access. Employees will forget to get them if they cannot do it at work, so it makes sense to bring the service onsite. At the same time, if the provider can give booster shots or other immunizations the employee would otherwise receive from the doctor – but at a lower price through the onsite provider – it makes sense to pay for it through the onsite provider (especially if you are self-funded). Don't forget to bring in the spouse and dependents!! You're paying for them anyway. Moreover, if you're fully funded, the chances are good that the onsite clinics can bill for your shots through your insurance providers.

- **Onsite Biometrics** – I've addressed this before as well, but if you are going to incorporate biometrics into your incentives, it makes sense to bring them onsite to provide convenience to your employees. Any time you can eliminate or reduce a barrier to entry or participation, you have a greater chance of higher engagement. Bringing biometrics onsite helps to make it easier. Making it open to the spouse to attend can also help to increase participation as well as reduce overall costs (vs. completing biometrics at the doctor).

- **Health Risk Assessment** – I have not discussed the health risk assessment sooner, although it is built into the online wellness platform. Following the passing of the Genetic Information in Employment Act (GINA), most companies have stripped down the Health Risk Assessment to the point that they provide very little practical or useful information. They ask a few good questions, but they do very little to provide predictive analysis to the individual.

We lean towards the biometrics to provide better information to assist the individual to plan for and change their behavior.

- **Discounted Gym Memberships and Subsidies** – Employers (either with or without an onsite gym) may offer discounts to local gyms. Most gyms will arrange special pricing to employers at no cost as a promotional opportunity to provide discount rates for employees. In other cases, employers may subsidize gym memberships for employees and their spouses to use local gyms. Smart employers require documentation of attendance at local gyms for continued receipt of the gym discounts (e.g., check-in sheets) as another motivational step to generate momentum for change.

- **Nurse Hotline** – In the section on telemedicine, I mention the Nurse Hotline or similar services. These services are still active and well used. Be sure to remind employees of their availability. These constant reminders of resources that are available may help them to remember what is possible when then need it again. Having the Nurse Hotline to call at 2 a.m. when your child is running a fever is a much better option than running him or her into the emergency room.

- **Musculoskeletal** – Back, neck, muscle, and joint issues are common among employees, and one of the most common reasons for employees to take time off. Discomfort and pain are common when facing these challenges. Collectively, employees may suffer from these conditions for years and never seek treatment, thereby exacerbating conditions year after year.

  New programs are available to employers working with musculoskeletal disorders, taking a clinical approach to evaluate the situation and determine the best method. Hinge Health is a company taking this approach delivering at-home care for joint and back pain. The 12-week treatment program includes behavioral health coaching, exercise therapy, wearable motion sensors to track movement, and personalized education. In the end, this has shown to improve outcomes for chronic knee pain by 61% and elective surgeries by 64%.

- **Expert Medical Opinion** – Employers who "get it" are offering Expert Medical Opinion (EMO) programs to individuals struggling with medical decisions who need their medical case reviewed by experts for assistance to determine next steps. Many times, patients do not have access to second opinions in the local market. Providing an EMO service allows employees access to additional expertise to confirm diagnosis and treatment plans or to offer alternative diagnosis or approaches. This may prevent unnecessary procedures and save costs. More importantly, it provides individuals the empowerment they need to access experts, education, and coordination with treating physicians.

- **Genomics / Gene Replacement / Stem Cell Therapy** – More employers are looking to non-traditional options to deal with conditions that were once only thought to be surgical to repair. Stem cell therapy, gene replacement, and other work in the areas of genomics appear to have the data to support new ideas that have merit. Rather than merely replacing knees, research is showing compelling evidence that demonstrates similar or better results in cell regeneration without the complications. Yes, I am the first of the group to say that I'll "believe it when I see it." The successes are stacking up and worth taking a keen look at now.

- **Reference-Based Pricing** - There has been a lot of buzz lately about reference-based pricing (RBP) as a potential solution to bring down the cost of healthcare. I'll bring it up here is a discussion point just so my critics don't tell me that I forgot to talk about it. It's not that I forgot about it – I'm not a believer of its feasibility in most markets. It's a concept that sounds good on paper but one that I have rarely seen executed well.

Here's a general concept. As we all know, the price is NEVER the price. The same procedure or service in healthcare could have 100 different price variations depending upon the situation, method of payment, insurance used, payer, payee, discounts, etc. When we use a network through our carrier, the price we receive from our provider is based upon the level of service we purchase to access the network available through our insurance provider.

As an employer, if I am big enough to apply pressure to a healthcare provider – just like the insurance companies – to get them to accept a lower amount for their services, wouldn't that be a good win? This practice's reimbursement at a percentage above Medicare's standard pricing to encourage employees to avoid doctors and facilities that charge above average prices for nonemergency services.

Strategies to Bend the Cost Curve

Need Help?

Come join the conversation!

Find more information about Wade Larson and ideas to improve your leadership functions at:

www.WadeLarson.com

Look for Other Titles

Continuous Improvement in HR

Sound impossible? It's not only possible, but necessary for you to find solutions to save time, energy and opportunity to stop spending time on the "stuff" so you can start spending more time on what matters most— PEOPLE. Get back to why you got into HR in the first place.

Available from the website or on Amazon.

Connect with Dr. Wade

 @DrWadeLarson   @DrWadeLarson

 @DrWadeLarson

Bring Dr. Wade into Your Next Event

- Keynotes
- Workshops
- Training
- Speaking Events

Go to www.WadeLarson.com for more info.

www.ingramcontent.com/pod-product-compliance
Lightning Source LLC
Chambersburg PA
CBHW060835170526
45158CB00001B/169